Intentional Catholic Family

Intentional Catholic Family

CREATING YOUR GROWTH PLAN FOR A PURPOSE-FILLED YEAR

Julianne M. Will

Our Sunday Visitor
Huntington, Indiana

Nihil Obstat
Msgr. Michael Heintz, Ph.D.
Censor Librorum

Imprimatur
✠ Kevin C. Rhoades
Bishop of Fort Wayne-South Bend
May 18, 2023

The *Nihil Obstat* and *Imprimatur* are official declarations that a book is free from doctrinal or moral error. It is not implied that those who have granted the *Nihil Obstat* and *Imprimatur* agree with the contents, opinions, or statements expressed.

28 27 26 25 24 23   1 2 3 4 5 6 7 8 9

Our Sunday Visitor Publishing Division
Our Sunday Visitor, Inc.
200 Noll Plaza
Huntington, IN 46750
www.osv.com
1-800-348-2440

ISBN: 978-1-68192-726-8 (Inventory No. T2598)
1. RELIGION—Christian Living—Family & Relationships.
2. FAMILY & RELATIONSHIPS—Activities.
3. RELIGION—Christianity—Catholic.

eISBN: 978-1-68192-727-5

Cover design: Tyler Ottinger
Cover art: Adobestock
Interior design: Amanda Falk

PRINTED IN THE UNITED STATES OF AMERICA

Introduction

A friend whom I follow on social media has always talked about her family as her "team." So you'll see adorable photos of her with her husband, daughter, and son captioned, "Celebrating a Team Jones tradition with a trip to our favorite beach!" or "Big hockey weekend for Team Jones!" (Not their real last name, but you get the idea.) I've always been a little bit envious of that. It's clear that they're firmly united by a strong family identity.

"Team" wasn't how I grew up. My parents, my two sisters, and I always pulled together to do what we needed to do. But we didn't have this idea of kids and parents being on the same side. I think many Gen-Xers would agree that when we were kids and teens, parents were the punchline, or the very enemy of "cool." Us and them. Definitely not part of a team.

And then I found myself a single mom of just one. My daughter's father and I divorced right after her first birthday. I was granted an annulment several years later, but I didn't remarry and have more children. Not for lack of wanting; somehow, it just didn't happen.

Life was sometimes a struggle. I worked all the time to make ends meet. My daughter was alone a lot, even when I was home, or with camp directors and after-school caregivers. I managed the house and car, handled the bills, scheduled doctors' visits and parent-teacher conferences, did the laundry, and shopped for the groceries. All the things!

School was hard (my sweet daughter has ADHD). So were things at home, where she had a fair number of responsibilities. We made time for traditions (Sunday pancakes! Half birthdays!) and did all kinds of fun things in our community. But we were less like a team and more like exhausted warriors in The Great Eternal Fight to Keep Up with It All — a battle we were always losing.

My little party of two was different not only from my friend's "team," but also from the type of family to which my then-parish ministered. I remember reaching out in search of a community of single parents. I explained my circumstances — ten-year-old daughter, full-time day job. After getting bounced from voicemail to voicemail over the course of many weeks, I finally got a call back from a woman who invited me to join the moms' group for parents of *toddlers*. They met once a week in the mornings. Well, that wasn't gonna work! I was told there wasn't anything for single working parents of older kids, and my offers to initiate something fell upon deaf ears. It was a little soul-crushing.

Fast forward fifteen years to Christmas 2019, when I found myself copy editing a book containing the presentations from a symposium called *Renewing Catholic Family Life*. It had been organized by renowned author and psychologist Dr. Gregory K. Popcak (founder and executive director of the Pastoral Solutions Institute), and featured some of the most diverse, studied, and dynamic writers and scholars in today's US Catholic Church.

I felt encouraged when I read real-life statistics about today's Catholic families and saw myself; particularly because today's nontraditional Catholic family was presented not as a failure, but rather an evolution that requires support. It was a relief to hear Catholic leaders discuss ways to help nontraditional families avoid further ruptures and to heal, instead of browbeating or excluding them. It was valuable to see the US Church's thought leaders invite diverse voices to speak out; to take a fact-based look at the composition of the Church; and to ask questions about how the Church could do better. I felt particularly inspired by Dr. William Keimig and Dr. Julie Hanlon Rubio, who urge greater love and unity in the Church, and encourage practical ways of thinking about Catholic families as they exist in the real world.

Dr. Rubio wrote:

> In (Catholic social thought), families are called the first cell of society, domestic churches, and schools of virtue where, ideally, children and adults learn how to be good people, faithful Catholics, and active citizens. Catholic teaching understands family as a crucial part of the social order and a key to the creation of a civilization of love. Yet the potential of this thinking remains unrealized due to insufficient attention to the practical questions of daily life and counterproductive ideological and cultural divides in the Church.[1]

When parents are faced with a nebulous call to raise good people, faithful Catholics, and active citizens without a specific "how," or they see an idealized goal that doesn't account for the reality of the practical questions of their daily life, it's easy to lose them — particularly if they're met with criticism for their state in life. Yet I believe that most parents don't treat divorce or busyness or their faith casually. I believe that most of us enter into family life with common goals and dreams, and that some are simply unable to achieve the ideal family due to mistakes, outside influences, addiction, illness, or a million other valid, heartbreaking reasons. We need a bit of realistic acceptance and a source of easy-to-implement ideas for teaching and doing with a way to organize it into our lives.

As it happened, I was copyediting the *Renewing Catholic Family Life* compilation shortly after my friend wished us all a Happy New Year from Team Jones, and right after I'd purchased a business journal-type book designed to help individuals set and achieve goals. It made me think: What if there were a way to apply the structure of goal setting to family faith and togetherness? A really practical guide to helping families achieve that sense of "team" … but a team shaped by Catholic values? What if families created a vision through which they could filter everything they do during the year — a vision aligned with Christ's vision?

What if we drilled down through the esoteric, the rhetoric, the broad admonishment to "do good and be good," and helped Catholic families find really specific ways to effect change, in their homes and in their communities? And why not use a practice familiar from business and everyday life — the discipline of crafting a mission statement, vision, and goals?

Sounds great, right? But could it work?

When I was a single working parent, I was B.U.S.Y. Thinking always came second to doing. There was no time to ponder or plan! Are you kidding?

And even though I spent years as a Catholic book editor, even though I was a religious education teacher for some very cute first graders one season, even though I grew up Catholic and attended Catholic grade school, I realized — maybe more than most — how *much* there is to know about the Faith. It's a lot to get your arms around.

I'm also acutely aware of how momentum can dwindle. I write about nutrition and fitness, too, and heaven only knows how many treadmills end up serving as expensive clothing racks.

So, this book is #goals. It's the perfection that you aim for, but will never truly achieve until you literally reach heaven. This book is designed to meet your family where you are, and to help you build the awareness, habits, and experiences that, over time, build the domestic church which can serve as a lifelong foundation for your children. It offers a step-by-step guide to intentionally forming a faith-aligned family mission and vision and identifying ways to achieve them … or at least come really close. (Every great team needs practice!) This can be an annual exercise, one that you refine after experience and modify based on your child's or children's growth. It can be as big or small as your family and your resources. And you can start — or restart — at any time of year.

THERE ARE MYRIAD WELL-KNOWN EXPERTS TEACHING ALL OF US HOW TO DEVELOP A MISSION AND VISION AND SET GOALS IN OUR CAREERS AND THE BUSINESS WORLD. SO WHY NOT LEARN FROM THEIR EXPERTISE AND APPLY IT TO THAT MOST IMPORTANT OF ORGANIZATIONS: OUR FAMILIES?

This approach should engage every family member as an important part of your team; you'll all work together to decide what you stand for, then get specific about how that'll guide you in all kinds of circumstances. It offers the best kind of belonging: to be a loved and valued part of a group with a clear identity and necessary role in the world.

And believe it or not, you're already halfway there. Because "you are no longer strangers and sojourners, but you are fellow citizens with the saints and members of the household of God, built upon the foundation of the apostles and prophets, Christ Jesus himself being the cornerstone, in whom the whole structure is joined together and grows into a holy temple in the Lord; in whom you are also built into it for a dwelling place of God in the Spirit" (Ephesians 2:19–22). You're already a part of God's family — you're a part of his team.

Now it's just a matter of building that same sort of structure within your home, so that you can take it back out into the world. There are myriad well-known experts teaching all of us how to develop a mission and vision and set goals in our careers and the business world. So why not learn from their expertise and apply it to that most important of organizations: our families?

WHAT DIFFERENCE DOES IT MAKE?

At the very beginning of *Renewing Catholic Family Life*, Dr. Popcak asks these impactful questions of the nation's faith leaders and family ministry professionals:

1. Are Catholic families called to relate differently to one another than our non-Catholic counterparts? If so, how?
2. What does an authentic "domestic-church-based spirituality" (i.e., one that doesn't simply try to shoehorn monastic practices into family life) look like in practice?
3. How can Catholic parents be more effective at practicing intentional discipleship at home and be equipped to raise the next generation of intentional disciples?
4. How can Catholic families be empowered to become the primary outposts of evangelization and positive social change that the Church calls them to be?

Big ideas. Great questions! You could start by simply asking: What difference does it make that our family is Catholic? Maybe you can't answer that right now. And that's OK. Most of us have been too busy living in said family to think much about it. My hope for you is that, as you use this book to walk through the processes that successfully help companies and businesspeople find unity and identity, you'll determine how your family is uniquely equipped and called to live your Catholic Faith and bring the radical love shown by Jesus to the world.

There are so many beautiful things about the Catholic Faith that I didn't really appreciate until I was an adult — things that have unexpectedly influenced my thinking about justice, community, neighbor, the planet, leadership, work, and other major aspects of being a part of humankind.

By working with your family to figure out your unique identity and live your best life together, as you were created to, you'll find greater closeness, a sense of team, and a place of refuge and love in your family that will serve you all for the rest of your lives.

PRAYER ATTRIBUTED TO ST. TERESA OF ÁVILA

Christ has no body now on earth but yours;
no hands but yours; no feet but yours.
Yours are the eyes through which the compassion of Christ must look out on the world.
Yours are the feet with which he is to go about doing good.
Yours are the hands with which he is to bless his people.

PARENTS: HOW TO USE THIS BOOK

If you're like me, you skip all of the introductory paragraphs and go right to bullet number 1. Just tell me what to do. Let's get down to brass tacks, right? You could do that here, but you'll probably be lost, your kids will probably be bored, and you'll all probably give up by week 3.

So just do this: Read over chapters 1 through 4. Dog-ear pages that you want to come back to, and make notes in the margins. Keep some sticky notes handy, in case you want to make a shopping list or jot down a to-do that needs to go on your refrigerator or in your planner.

Peek at week 1 in the workbook section, just so that you know what it looks like before you get there.

Then start bringing in your kids. Depending on their ages, you can let them read the chapter defining mission, vision, and goals directly. They might find it interesting and helpful for other parts of their lives. But if they're little, be ready to give them a sweeping overview, which might sound something like:

> Our family is going to work together as a team this year to do the things God wants us to do, and to learn more about being Catholic. You get to help choose the things that we're going to do. We're going to talk about what we're good at, and what we enjoy. And we're going to decide together how we want to make the world a better place.

If necessary, you might mention that this process will involve good snacks, stickers, lots of hugs and high fives, or some other motivation. Don't be afraid to sell it a little bit!

Choose a relatively quiet time of year in which to launch your program. You might need to have a family meeting before you get to week 1. You might need two. You do you!

Weeks 1 through 52 are your action weeks. I've included some stuff to discuss each week — some fun facts, some resources, and some education for those of us (me) who grew up Catholic but still didn't know enough to teach anyone else.

I've also included some encouragement. Motivational professionals get paid big bucks to come up with tips and tools for business success. Why not use their professional expertise to help us achieve our family goals? We might not think about our kids' "actual cost of work performed" or the "benefits realization" of identifying our vision, but there are fundamental project-management principles that work for the C-suite and the ABC set alike.

Finally, I've included a prayer each week. But don't let that be prescriptive. Feel free to use your own words; in fact, I encourage it. Talk to God as a family about what you need, what you've learned, what you're thankful or sorry for, or what's relevant in your life that week. Everything required to create a great prayer is already in your heart.

Most of all, use this book to feel empowered. I've simply offered a template.* It's the same thinking behind cookbooks, personal trainers, and learn-to-paint classes. A little direction and a schedule can do wonders for a nebulous good intention.

---

*On that note: My suggestions here for resources, including organizations and trips, do not represent endorsements or even recommendations. In fact, I've not had personal experience with every single resource that I list here. These only represent starting points to get your Google juices flowing.

The Best Laid Plans

Have you ever considered taking your family on a Great American Road Trip? You know, just like the movies: an upbeat playlist, endless byways and backroads, with opportunities for discovery around every corner. The wind in your hair and not a care in the world. Maps, schmaps. Let's see where the road takes us.

It's pure exhilaration, right?

Until it becomes a hot mess. Like when a hailstorm barrels over the horizon, there isn't a gas station for another four hours, and you ran out of gummy worms about 120 miles ago.

A slapdash plan (such as the kind typically preferred by one of the adults in our household who shall remain nameless) can have its pitfalls: If you'd checked first, you would have known that The World's Largest Truck Stop is closed for repaving, and that the campground you'd hoped to stay at is full.

Truly successful road trips are the result of detailed planning. Before the rubber meets the road, someone has doped out each roadside attraction and overnight stop along the way, confirmed that they're all open, and made reservations. Someone has stocked the car with not just snacks and water, but also emergency supplies for bad weather and breakdowns. Mileage has been tallied, the vehicle has been serviced, and clothes are packed for crazy weather. Maybe someone has even made a playlist.

And therein lies the opportunity for marvelous, magical discovery. Once you know where you're going and how you're going to get there, you can relax into the journey *with greater capacity* for observation and surprise.

If you've ever planned a vacation with your family, you probably know all this. A vision, goals, a plan, schedules, timelines — all are integral to a rewarding trip. They are also at the core of growing, successful companies; there's a reason these exercises are part of every business plan. And they're just as important for individuals — they form the basis for most successful New Year's resolutions, diet programs, and inspirational journals. Everyone, from personal money management guru Suze Orman to business consultant and motivational pro Stephen Covey, has recommended developing a personal or professional mission statement, vision, and goals.

So, if such tools drive a great road trip (pardon the pun), and provide a road map to the future for successful businesses (really, the puns are irresistible), why would you leave your family's spiritual journey to anything less?

Growing closer as a family to one another and to God requires intention. It necessitates learning about what our Catholic Faith calls us to do and to be, and then drafting a plan for how we each can strive toward that, given our unique and marvelous family structures, values, talents, and gifts.

There will be bumps in the road and detours, perhaps stormy days and delays (so many orange cones!). But with an itinerary formed by God's word in the Bible and the teachings of our faith tradition, we can set our sights on our ultimate goal — fulfilling his plan for our lives — and along the way realize the best of our time together.

This guide is designed to help you make that plan. We'll employ some traditional and contemporary business resources to help you draft a mission statement, vision, and goals for your family. We'll include some professional and educational tips and tricks to engage little ones and encourage solid habits. And with your loved ones, you'll grow in your family and faith identity. Rather than a lot of coming and going and mere surviving, you can satisfy your longing for a deep connection to your family; you can become a team, united in the extraordinary light and goodness that comes from living according to God's plan.

And I know you hear this all the time, but that's because it's true: Time with our sweet kiddos is all too brief, friends. When you consider quality time, you want to be sure that it includes the development of that most important relationship: your children's relationship with God. As Pope Francis expressed it:

> In the family, faith accompanies every age of life, beginning with childhood: children learn to trust in the love of their parents. This is why it is so important that within their families parents encourage shared expressions of faith which can help children gradually to mature in their own faith.[1]

This book is designed to help you create those "shared expressions of faith" in an intentional way unique to your family.

ARE WE THERE YET?

As a single working mom, I didn't take many road trips with my daughter. Sure, we did lots of things — free days at art museums, summer camps while I was at the office, community events, restaurant excursions. One adult plus one child makes you fairly mobile, even if the budget is tight.

But these experiences were part of a massively overscheduled existence. I was constantly working, or I was mowing the lawn, buying the groceries, cleaning the house, scheduling the doctor visits, and helping with homework. I even managed to squeeze in some volunteer responsibilities, trips to the gym, and occasional nights out with friends. Quite frankly, it was ridiculous.

I look back and wonder whether my darling little girl — a chatterbox who struggled with ADHD — really enjoyed all of those family festivals and concerts at the park. Was I fully present? Had I screamed at her to hurry up on the way to our "happy afternoon fun"? Was any of it serving my goals of spending quality time with my daughter, exposing her to new experiences, and broadening her mind? Were those even worthy goals?

Most of us as parents want similar things for our children: We want them to enjoy a full, well-rounded life. To never lack the essentials. To have interesting experiences that challenge their minds, and healthy experiences that challenge their bodies. We want our children to be good, capable, kind people, who can function on their own and one day enter into heaven.

But do we ever stop to think about how we'll get there?

I'd venture to say that unexamined busyness is not unique to my family, nor even single parents. Sometimes, in fact, busyness expands to fill one's capacity. Yet, without thinking about our mission as a family, and then identifying a vision for how we'll be in the world, with goals to serve as signposts of progress … how do we know when we've arrived?

THE KEY TO AVOIDING FURTHER BUSYNESS? DON'T LET THIS EFFORT TO BE A MORE INTENTIONAL CATHOLIC FAMILY BECOME JUST ONE MORE THING. MAKE IT THE FIRST THING, AND LET ALL OF THE OTHERS FOLLOW FROM IT.

This is the beauty of carving out time to develop your family's faith identity, just as surely as you carve out time for birthday parties and basketball practice: You know how to tell when you're on track.

The key to avoiding further busyness? Don't let this effort to be a more intentional Catholic family become just one more thing. *Make it the first thing, and let all of the others follow from it.* Filter your family's decisions about how you use your time and resources through the mission, vision, and goals that you set together. (*Together* being key, as we'll talk about later.)

Once you've identified your destination and your stops along the way, it'll be *so* much easier to determine whether an activity or event fits into that plan. Does it further your goals and bring you closer to your vision? Does it honor your mission?

DODGING DETOURS

Saying no can be hard. I worry quite a bit about disappointing others, or — even worse — failing to meet my own expectations. It becomes a whole lot easier, however, if I know that I've already created a plan that meets God's expectations and strengthens my family. I've constructed some guard rails.

How you or I go about doing that might change from day to day or year to year. Sometimes you may need to focus your energies on a pressing need within your family, and sometimes you may be able to direct more of those resources toward your community. Recognizing that the goals you and your family establish may need to expand or contract is crucial to success (and sanity).

But having some sort of parameter helps guide those decisions. Because, to use our road trip analogy, if you realize that a mediocre roadside attraction is going to take you 330 miles off course and force you to give up a really important stop on your trip, then crossing it off the list is a pretty simple choice.

When thinking about your family's mission, vision, and goals, it's important to keep priorities clear. FranklinCovey, world-renowned for its expertise in leadership and management, speaks of balance this way: "To live a more balanced existence, you have to recognize that not doing everything that comes along is okay. There's no need to overextend yourself. All it takes is realizing that it's all right to say no when necessary and then focus on your highest priorities."[2]

What your family decides to say yes to can be wildly personal. Basketball practice may help your kids fulfill your family's goal of caring for your health as God's creation. A birthday party may be an important part of growing a community within your neighborhood or city. I'm not here to dictate a prescriptive list of right and wrong choices for your family. This practice of developing a mission, vision, and goals is an outline that will help your family consider what's best for *your* family and how those choices fit into a thoughtful, loving plan that you've drafted together with God and our faith in mind.

Hey, if you think that roadside attraction 330 miles out of the way will be a fantastic part of your overall journey and fits right in with the theme of your trip, then turn on the blinker!

So, let's figure out where you're going and how you're going to get there. Parenting is a big job, and as the *Catechism of the Catholic Church* makes clear, leading our children to a relationship with God and all that that entails is one of our primary roles:

- "Parents have the first responsibility for the education of their children. They bear witness to this responsibility first by *creating a home* where tenderness, forgiveness, respect, fidelity, and disinterested service are the rule." (2223)
- "*Education in the faith* by the parents should begin in the child's earliest years. … Parents have the mission of teaching their children to pray and to discover their vocation as children of God." (2226)

No pressure, right? It might seem intimidating, until you realize that you can learn *right alongside your kids.*

PROGRESS, NOT PERFECTION

Keep in mind that this process of creating a mission, a vision, and goals isn't a top-down, hard-and-fast, fail-or-succeed kind of experience. Instead, help your family to embrace the growth mindset espoused by Carol Dweck, an author, speaker, researcher, and professor of psychology at Stanford

University: "Individuals who believe their talents can be developed (through hard work, good strategies, and input from others) have a growth mindset," Dweck writes.[3] "They tend to achieve more than those with a more fixed mindset (those who believe their talents are innate gifts). This is because they worry less about looking smart and they put more energy into learning."

I first learned of Dweck's work when my daughter's college-prep high school introduced the growth mindset philosophy to parents and students. The school's director encouraged us to reward not just achievement, but also the strategy, work, and perseverance it took to get there. A growth mindset transforms the meaning of difficulty from "roadblock" to "learning opportunity."

At the same time, this isn't just another participation award: "Unproductive effort is never a good thing," Dweck says. "It's critical to reward not just effort but learning and progress, and to emphasize the processes that yield these things, such as seeking help from others, trying new strategies, and capitalizing on setbacks to move forward effectively."

So together, as a team of kids and grown-ups, try to view your family's mission, vision, and goals through what Dweck describes as "the power of yet" — the power of believing that you can improve.[4] After all, that's how God views all of us works in progress: with an overflowing, never-ending measure of grace. And thank God, right?!

DESTINATION JOY

Our Sunday Visitor gave me my first FranklinCovey planner when I started there as a book editor way back in 2001. Believe it or not, I'm still using the same black leather binder more than twenty years later. It's been so integral to my organizational strategy that my daughter says the sound of its zipper is part of the soundtrack of her life; after all, she's been hearing it since she was four.

I've lived and died by thousands of days' worth of to-do lists within those pages. But I failed to really absorb the *purpose* of Stephen Covey's planning tools. I was so busy tackling tasks that I didn't have time to think, to contemplate … to plan! In focusing on productivity, I missed the point: Why do anything if it's not serving a larger mission for our lives, taking us closer to a vision that aligns with our "best selves" — those human beings whom God created us to be, making full use of the talents with which he's imbued us to bring his love to our families, our communities, and our world?

"Goals can take considerable effort to accomplish. So before you set them in stone, take a step back and figure out the 'life case' for choosing this goal on which to work," writes Kory Kogon, FranklinCovey's vice president of field development.[5] "Lock yourself in a room and ask, 'Why do it? Why is it important to me, my work, or my family? If I achieve the goal, what will the return be to me and those around me?'"

Back to this hypothetical road trip that you're now planning (with an ample supply of trail mix, please!). In deciding where you want to go, you probably have to take a few stops off the list, whether for a lack of time, money, or collective interest. If you're like me, this is hard, because you want to DO IT ALL. It's unrealistic, of course, to do it all, but very hard to peel back … until you realize that doing so leaves more time for the things that you really love and that make a difference for your family, your community, and your world, bringing you closer to God's vision for your life.

Making time to intentionally plan *with* and *for* your family will free you from the constant decision making that can lead you to lose your way, possibly missing out on the best "yes" of all: the joy of feeling aligned with your family and the purpose for which you were created. "For we are his workmanship, created in Christ Jesus for good works, which God prepared beforehand, that we should walk in them" (Ephesians 2:10).

So, take a few moments now to make notes about things in your own family life that you want to keep, and things that you want to add, delete, or change. Or consider what James Clear, the author of the productivity book *Atomic Habits,* writes: "Which areas of (your) life are in maintenance mode? Which areas are in growth mode?"[6]

PRAYER

Dear God, please share your wisdom with us as we start this process of shaping our family life to look more like your vision for us. And please send your Holy Spirit to provide courage, patience, and inspiration in our thoughts, words, and actions. Thank you for your grace and love! Amen.

Did You Know Your Family Is Church?

Before we move on to crafting a family mission and vision statement, let's take a minute to understand why it's so important to do this as a family. Your role is much bigger than perhaps you might realize. In Catholic circles, among Church leaders, parish directors of religious education, priests, and even the pope, families are referred to as the "domestic church."

That comes with a lot of respect and reverence. The Church, in her wisdom, recognizes that faith starts in the home, and it's lived out via the family. Yet many families have never even heard of the phrase *domestic church*. How do you act as the domestic church if you don't know that you are the domestic church?

It's a pretty big responsibility, as well as an honor. So let's break it down.

Lumen Gentium, one of the documents that came out of the Second Vatican Council,[1] says, "The family is, so to speak, the domestic church. In it parents should, by their word and example, be the first preachers of the faith to their children; they should encourage them in the vocation which is proper to each of them, fostering with special care vocation to a sacred state."[2]

And in the *Catechism*, the domestic church is described thus: "'The Christian family constitutes a specific revelation and realization of ecclesial communion, and for this reason it can and should be called a *domestic church*.' It is a community of faith, hope, and charity; it assumes singular importance in the Church, as is evident in the New Testament" (2204).

Sometimes people have a vision of what this must look like. Surely, a Catholic family as the domestic church must include a mother, father, and many children, all well-behaved. They all pray before bedtime every night, and they all gather for a lovely dinner every evening, especially on Sundays. Of course, they never watch TV or listen to mainstream music. They're separate from society and today's culture, a happy and kind microcosm in their well-kept home.

And if this describes your family, well, that's a beautiful thing, right up to the part about being separate from society and today's culture. But it's also pretty unrealistic for most of us.

I appreciate what Dr. Timothy O'Malley, director of the Notre Dame Center for Liturgy at the McGrath Institute for Church Life, has written on the matter:

> This romanticized account of family life tends to bypass the experience of actual families. It is an almost idolatrous vision of family life that passes over the difficulties that a family will experience in becoming a civilization of love. There are families suffering from the plague of domestic violence. Some couples are unable to have children, experiencing the agony of infertility rather than the communion that leads to a large brood of Catholic children singing along to the *Salve Regina*. In the United States, migrant families are separated, attempting to make a life apart from each other — sometimes by choice and sometimes because of political policy. Families in the United States suffer from poverty, unable to keep a roof over their heads let alone enjoy a meal together. Parents agonize as their children are arrested, struggle with alcohol and drug addiction, experience divorce, and even die prematurely. If the term "domestic church" is to function prophetically within society, it must take [in] the fullness of the human condition — not only an idealized, upper middle-class account of Christian life.[3]

Can I get an amen?

It hearkens back to my own experience as a single mom in a little domestic church of two, ruled by a crazy work schedule and dogged by difficulty in getting through the day, let alone fulfilling the expectations for a Catholic family within my parish. We aren't all the perfect blend of *Leave It to Beaver* and *The Sound of Music*.

Fortunately, our popes over the decades have described a much more measured, realistic, and welcoming view of the family. In *Familiaris Consortio* (On the Role of the Christian Family in the Modern World), published in 1981, Pope St. John Paul II devotes a section to "The Situation of the Family in the World Today," describing specific social struggles that were, in large part, still present when Pope Francis wrote his chapter on "The Experiences and Challenges of Families" in his work *Amoris Laetitia* (On Love in the Family), published in 2016.

Julie Hanlon Rubio summarizes these well:

> *Amoris Laetitia* continues the trajectory set in motion by Leo XIII and Saint John Paul II. Oppressive social forces acting upon families named in *Amoris Laetitia* include both problematic ways of thinking and harmful social structures. Pope Francis worries about "an extreme individualism which weakens family bonds" and encourages families not to be "caught up with possessions and pleasures." He connects the "throwaway culture," in

which we buy things only to discard them when new things come along, to a temporary marriage culture in which partners are abandoned when they fail to satisfy. These pervasive ways of thinking can limit individuals' capacities to choose marriage and fidelity to their families. Francis also identifies problematic social structures that hurt families, including: insufficient affordable housing; a failure to recognize family rights (including the just wage); a failure to adequately respond to violence against and sexual exploitation of women and children; economic situations that drive migration and trafficking; and inadequate support for single parents living in poverty. Like Leo XIII, Francis realizes that there are forces beyond families' control that make their life difficult, attends to sources of their brokenness, and lifts up the potential of all families to be "light in the darkness of the world."[4]

FOUR FOUNDATIONAL FAMILY ROLES

Popes John Paul II and Francis both acknowledge some of the inevitable and even extraordinary difficulties that families face. And their guidance for creating a domestic church has less to do with the size, skin color, or socioeconomic status of our family, and a lot more to do with how we treat one another and the world around us. In fact, part of our role as a domestic church is to assist those outside of our immediate family who are facing these kinds of challenges.

In *Familiaris Consortio*, Pope St. John Paul II writes:

> Thus, with love as its point of departure and making constant reference to it, the recent synod emphasized four general tasks for the family:
>
> 1) forming a community of persons;
> 2) serving life;
> 3) participating in the development of society;
> 4) sharing in the life and mission of the Church.[5]

Not a bad outline for your family's mission statement, is it? In the next couple of chapters, we're going to walk through how to execute this idea of a family mission. We'll add your family's vision statement, which will describe how your home, your community, and the world will look because you have lived out your mission statement. We'll identify goals — the concrete, actual steps that you take to achieve numbers one through four.

In *Amoris Laetitia*, Pope Francis touches on these four tasks of the family as he describes the internal and external roles we should strive for as family members. He articulates beautiful ways of being. Note, I didn't say "things to do," but "ways to be." First, the internal ways of being:

> It is a profound spiritual experience to contemplate our loved ones with the eyes of God and to see Christ in them. This demands a freedom and openness which enable us to appreciate their dignity. We can be fully present to others only by giving fully of ourselves and forgetting all else. Our loved ones merit our complete attention. Jesus is our model in

> this, for whenever people approached to speak with him, he would meet their gaze, directly and lovingly (cf. Mk 10:21). No one felt overlooked in his presence, since his words and gestures conveyed the question: "What do you want me to do for you?" (Mk 10:51). This is what we experience in the daily life of the family. We are constantly reminded that each of those who live with us merits complete attention, since he or she possesses infinite dignity as an object of the Father's immense love. This gives rise to a tenderness which can "stir in the other the joy of being loved. Tenderness is expressed in a particular way by exercising loving care in treating the limitations of the other, especially when they are evident."

Family is not an insular experience in the Catholic Faith, however. There also are expectations for external efforts:

> Led by the Spirit, the family circle is not only open to life by generating it within itself, but also by going forth and spreading life by caring for others and seeking their happiness. This openness finds particular expression in hospitality, which the word of God eloquently encourages: "Do not neglect to show hospitality to strangers, for thereby some have entertained angels unawares" (Heb 13:2). When a family is welcoming and reaches out to others, especially the poor and the neglected, it is "a symbol, witness and participant in the Church's motherhood." … The family lives its spirituality precisely by being at one and the same time a domestic church and a vital cell for transforming the world.[6]

From these "ways to be," your family can then find the things that you will do that are specific to your family, using your God-given gifts. Think about how many ways you can show hospitality, for example. You might be the family that makes delicious meals for a sick neighbor, because you all love to cook and are good at it. Or you might be the family that coordinates the meal schedule, because your talents lend themselves to planning and organization.

FAMILY IS SAYING YES DURING THE VERY WORST TIMES IN LIFE. AND IN THIS WAY, IT MIRRORS WHAT CHRIST DID FOR US. THAT IS HOW IT BECOMES THE DOMESTIC CHURCH.

Families are powerful and special, and they occupy a unique role in the world. I really like the way Dr. O'Malley distinguishes family from affinity. Affinity is a shared experience or interest. It's hanging out, having fun together, friendship. Affinity is a wonderful, necessary, valuable tie between humans. But it's different from family. Family is obligation. Family is commitment that extends beyond the good times. Family is a parent working two full-time jobs to provide the necessities for his or her children. Family is cleaning the clothes and body of your spouse who is angry, sick, and in pain during cancer treatment.

Family is saying yes during the very worst times in life. And in this way, it mirrors what Christ did for us. That is how it becomes the domestic church. "Family life is that space where the divine drama of love becomes present amid the mundane," Dr. O'Malley writes.

And then, because this lesson of love and duty is so powerfully learned at home, it is naturally extended to the world at large. *The domestic church isn't insular.* God didn't create us to exist in little isolated pods, just taking care of ourselves and our own. The purpose of the domestic church is to teach us how to grow up and interrelate with humanity as a whole. We're all God's children on this whole gorgeous planet, and so we're called to extend our "yes" to all of his creation, just as Christ did. We have a responsibility to others, made clear in the Beatitudes and many other places in the Bible. Here again is another way to *be*; what you *do* is entirely specific to your family.

Pope Francis encourages us: "Let us dream, then, as a single human family, as fellow travelers sharing the same flesh, as children of the same earth which is our common home, each of us bringing the richness of his or her beliefs and convictions, each of us with his or her own voice, brothers and sisters all."[7] It's pretty big stuff, being a part of a family. But before we get lost in concepts, let's put some things down on paper, shall we?

A PRAYER FOR OUR DOMESTIC CHURCH

Dear God, please give me the energy to be lovingly aware of and present to the community of persons within my family. Please give me the knowledge and humility necessary to best foster within our home the kind of society that Jesus described. And please give me the courage to lead my family in carrying his love, peace, kindness, generosity, joy, gentleness, and faithfulness into the world at large. Amen.

A Few Quick Definitions

A mission statement, vision, goals ... even in corporate settings, these terms get thrown around loosely and used incorrectly all the time. So before we try to establish them, let's first make sure we know exactly what we're talking about.

THE MISSION STATEMENT

The encyclopedia at Entrepreneur.com says this: "A mission statement defines what an organization is, why it exists, its reason for being."

Your family mission statement describes who you are and what you're all about, collectively, today. Many mission statements are short and sweet. The T-shirt brand Life Is Good is very succinct: "To spread the power of optimism."

The description Catholic Charities has on its site is a bit more detailed:

> As Catholic Charities, we labor in the streets inviting and serving those who have been left out to know and experience the tremendous and abundant love of God through Jesus Christ. We commit ourselves to break down walls of division that keep sisters and brothers separated from one another, excluded, or rendered disposable by our society. With joy, we resolve to build bridges of hope, mercy and justice toward the creation of a culture of communal care responsive to the cries of those who are poor.

Of course, the best family mission statement is the one that you create *with* your family, *for* your family; we'll walk through how to do that shortly. But for now, it may help to think of this as your baseline, your platform, your *who* you are and *why* you are. For what did God create you?

THE VISION STATEMENT

At BusinessDictionary.com, a vision statement is defined as "an aspirational description of what an organization would like to achieve or accomplish in the mid-term or long-term future. It is intended to serve as a clear guide for choosing current and future courses of action."

If a mission statement describes who you are and what you're here to do, then a vision statement describes how the world looks when you achieve that. You might also think of a mission statement as the ground floor, and a vision statement as the top floor. (And your goals, which we talk about next, are the stairs to get you there.)

Teach for America's vision statement is positively inspirational: "Together, we are driving impact across the country to achieve our vision that one day all children in this nation will have the opportunity to attain an excellent education."

To see how a mission leads to a vision, consider how Catholic Charities' vision flows from its mission: "Catholic Charities USA was founded over a century ago by men and women who believed that *the collective efforts of the church to faithfully serve people in need could change the course of poverty in our nation*" (emphasis added).

Isn't that beautiful? They describe their work with the poor in their mission, and they describe a sea of change in the future of the poor in their vision. First, who they are, what they do, and why they exist; then, the change that they want to effect in the world by their existence.

Your family's vision statement can represent an incremental achievement compared with where you are today … or it can take you all the way to heaven. It can change from year to year, as your children grow and your family life evolves. Whatever the case, it can and should be lofty. Dream big! What will the members of your family, your community, and your world look like because you were here and fulfilled your mission? What's different?

THE GOALS

Here's where the rubber meets the road. Goals should be specific, measurable, and attainable. They likely will have numbers and dates attached. Setting goals and tracking your progress is the only way you can know whether you're actually achieving your vision.

In other words, goals are the stairsteps taking you from your mission statement on the ground floor to your vision at the top.

This example from outdoor goods manufacturer and retailer Patagonia — "We will use only renewable or recycled materials in our products by 2025" — clearly outlines *what* to measure (how much of their products are made from renewable or recycled materials) and *when* (by 2025).[1]

You can find a detailed example of goal setting from the US Conference of Catholic Bishops in their document *Go and Make Disciples: A National Plan and Strategy for Catholic Evangelization in the United States*. Available online at USCCB.org, part 2 of the document lists not only specific goals, but also even more specific strategies. This is ideal for avoiding overwhelm and plotting out the smaller steps to get to the larger goals.

We'll discuss goal setting more specifically in a bit, but keep in mind Carol Dweck's growth mindset (discussed in chapter 1): You don't have to hit every goal on your first try, as long as you learn what works and what doesn't, and make progress toward your vision. We're going to talk about habits, too, and learn why they're crucial to goals.

We're All Friends Here

I'm sure you love your family. That's why you're here!

But how much do you *like* your family?

When you're working with colleagues to develop a mission statement, vision, and goals, everyone has to be polite. (Or they should be.) Meetings are scheduled with everyone's time in mind; there are roles; and there are ground rules. Sometimes, your company even provides lunch or snacks.

Approach this process at home with no less respect … and a lot more joy. Think about how you'll share ideas together within your family — maybe you'll need time limits, or maybe you'll need to require everyone to participate (even and especially your very cool, very busy teens). Consider solutions for alternative thinkers and different ages. Brainstorm ways to create a welcoming space where everyone can regularly gather.

And don't forget to discuss how to bring energy to this process. Food? Music? Matching T-shirts? Decorations? Rosaries for everyone? This is exciting! Find opportunities to make it fun (and ways to prevent anyone from making fun of anyone else).

Nailing the structure of your team adventure is pretty crucial to the whole process, so let's take some advice from the pros.

TIP 1: TAKE STEPS TO PREP

Be ready to razzle-dazzle in your first family meeting. If anything about this smells even faintly of a chore or a bore to your kids, you'll have lost before you start. Be prepared. In fact, consider not calling it a "meeting." (Soiree? Jamboree? Power hour?)

And stick to one big idea at your first get-together. This is not the time to develop your entire mission statement, vision statement, and goals. This is the time to talk about how you're going on an exciting journey together, learning how to make sure that the things you do line up with God's plan for your family team. Explain that you're going to identify what's important to your family, and what you're all really good at. Point out that everyone has a say in it. As Kristi Hedges, executive coach, leadership development consultant, speaker, and author of *The Power of Presence* and *The Inspiration Code,* wrote in *Forbes* magazine: "Real buy-in involves at least some element of co-creation. It invites discussion, debate, and allows everyone to feel even more vested in the outcome."[1]

TIP 2: KEEP IT SHORT

Education experts estimate kids' attention spans as age-plus-two-minutes. All kinds of things can influence this, too: time of day, hunger, distractions. Knowing your own children and their abilities, plan something for when they're rested, fed, and easily engaged. But always keep it shorter than you think. Rehearse what you're going to say and time it.

And if you go longer than fifteen minutes in any of your family huddles, change the pace or the activity. In the *Time* magazine article "How to Get — and Keep — Someone's Attention," author Annie Murphy Paul describes two studies that show how students' interest waxes and wanes as the stimulus changes. Learn from the hard-won insights of educators and keep things moving to keep your kids alert and involved.[2]

Dr. Joseph White, a clinical psychologist and frequent author and speaker on catechesis (religious education), has a tip for teachers that could work for parents as well: "Make the key concept the password," he writes.[3] Use a key phrase throughout your discussion on a particular topic. When you're ready to end your family get-together, ask your kids to repeat the key phrase as their password to leave.

TIP 3: ENGAGE THE SENSES

Jesus was the ultimate storyteller. He used parables all the time to convey memorable messages to the adults around him. So, take a page from the Bible and begin with a story.

Don't be afraid to use technology, too. See, for example, the Catholic Kids Media channel on YouTube. Short videos illustrate weekly readings, guided prayer, and sing-along hymns. (Many are available in Spanish, too.) The animated Brother Francis DVD series provides a fun introduction to a number of topics, including the sacraments. You can find these DVDs at brotherfrancis.com. Or for older kids, check out the Life Teen channel on YouTube, with fresh, modern approaches to current affairs, movies, tradition, teachings, and some Q&A that you'll likely find pretty fascinating as well.

And for each of your family soirees, try to tap into all the senses, just as Catholic liturgy does. Some ideas for you and your children to consider:

- Designate a spot where you'll get together. Think about how you can make it special. Maybe everyone sits on pillows?
- Candles add a warm ambiance, too.
- Clapping and hand-holding, sitting and standing are great transition actions.
- Or maybe everyone dances at the beginning or end of each session!
- This would be a great time to make sure everyone has a rosary.
- Matching T-shirts might be fun, too. (Especially once you've developed a mission or vision statement that could be printed, in part, on said shirts.)
- Consider adding a cross to your space, as well as a statue of Our Lady of Guadalupe, or Saint Francis, or another favorite saint.
- An elaborate retablo or a simple poster can set the scene. In fact, creating a retablo or poster together could be a part of your discussion about your mission, vision, or goals.
- Music can be the focus, or it can provide a background. If you'd like traditional Catholic music, https://greatcatholicmusic.com/ is a handy streaming service.
- You can also make your own music, with drums, bells, and singing. Or bass guitar. Why not?
- Incense has always been one of my favorite parts of special Masses, and you might consider making it a part of your family huddle.
- This might be time for a favorite snack. Woo them with treats!
- Or, you could hold your meetings/get-togethers/conversations while cooking together — just keep notebooks and pens at the ready for ideas.
- From the work world, you could steal the idea of walking meetings, in which colleagues head outside for a stroll while they discuss updates. Recording your conversation frees you from staying seated. (More on this in a bit.)

What else will you need? At least for that first get-together, make sure everyone has something to write with and something to write on. Crayons, markers, and glitter pens are all valid! Giving your notorious interrupters (big and small) a place to jot down notes is a great way to help them hold on to thoughts until it's their turn to speak.

If you have a family member who doesn't or can't write, or who communicates better verbally, you can designate a note-taker to capture his or her ideas, or you can record his or her thoughts with the video function on a cell phone or using an app like Otter.

Learners on the autism spectrum may appreciate a message conveyed within the context of an existing passion. Is your child's special interest Legos? Why not build models of concepts, or ask your child to build a model illustrating a story or theme?

A whiteboard, a chalkboard, or paper on an easel might be useful for jotting down notes during group discussions or brainstorming.

A big calendar with lots of space for writing is useful for plotting progress and scheduling activities. Or you could use an online calendar that everyone can sync, if your kids are older.

A Bible (or Bibles) will be essential.[4] You might have one for the family, or one for each member. You can use children's Bibles, or use an app. A copy of the *Catechism of the Catholic Church* will be important too; order a print copy or use an online version (you can find English versions available online for free at Vatican.va or USCCB.org).

Educators refer to the use of several styles of communication as multimodal teaching, and they employ it for good reason: It helps messages stick. So don't just talk to your kids. Talk *with* your kids. Make up songs. Sing and dance. Walk together. Watch videos. Write books or poems or haikus. Get out a hammer and nails. (Saint Joseph was a carpenter, after all. This could even lead to a goal of building a home with Habitat for Humanity in the coming year!)

WITHIN GOD'S WORD AND THE TEACHINGS OF THE FAITH, THERE IS AMPLE ROOM FOR YOUR BRAND OF FAMILY TO SHINE.

Embrace your differences. Let your kids lead. Celebrate your culture or ethnicity. *Catholicism is international, ancient, and diverse.* Within God's word and the teachings of the Faith (which we'll learn more about together in the coming year, if you're a little rusty), there is ample room for your brand of family to *shine.*

TIP 4: ESTABLISH GROUND RULES

There are lots of ways to address the rules of engagement for your family together time. But above all else: Ask your children to help. Getting their buy-in means greater compliance.

You could start with your usual family rules. Perhaps in your home, you've already established a good set of guidelines for conversational give and take, and you all work together well. But if you need to beef up the collaboration etiquette in your household (like many of us), consider these suggestions.

ALL THE LAW

This is really the mic-drop rule. I mean, if we all followed this rule to the best of our abilities, we wouldn't need any others. Jesus was succinct:

> And one of them, a lawyer, asked him a question, to test him. "Teacher, which is the great commandment in the law?" And he said to him, "You shall love the Lord your God with all your heart, and with all your soul, and with all your mind. This is the great and first commandment. And a second is like it, You shall love your neighbor as yourself. On these two commandments depend all the law and the prophets." (Matthew 22:35–40)

Probably the most concrete part of this for children is loving one's neighbor as oneself. It's easy in any given circumstance to ask, *How would you like that? How would you prefer to be treated? How would you want someone to respond if you were in that situation?*

Ideally, you can stop right there, and just weigh each questionable instance against this measuring stick: *Does that behavior show that I love God? Does it show that I love my neighbor? Would I like that for myself?*

THE TEN COMMANDMENTS

But if you need to be more concrete, there are the Ten Commandments:[5]

1. I am the Lord your God: you shall not have strange Gods before me.
2. You shall not take the name of the Lord your God in vain.
3. Remember to keep holy the Lord's Day.
4. Honor your father and your mother.
5. You shall not kill.
6. You shall not steal.
7. You shall not commit adultery.
8. You shall not bear false witness against your neighbor.
9. You shall not covet your neighbor's wife.
10. You shall not covet your neighbor's goods.

OSV has a book that breaks these down for children, since most kiddos won't relate to bearing false witness or coveting their neighbor's wife: *Living the 10 Commandments for Children,* by Rosemarie Gortler and Donna Piscitelli.

THE BEATITUDES

Sometimes, telling children what *to* do instead of what *not* to do works better. Giving them a model to aspire to fills the void left by the "shall nots." The Beatitudes are a beautiful expression of living the most important commandment:

> Seeing the crowds, [Jesus] went up on the mountain, and when he sat down his disciples came to him. And he opened his mouth and taught them, saying:
> "Blessed are the poor in spirit, for theirs is the kingdom of heaven.
> "Blessed are those who mourn, for they shall be comforted.
> "Blessed are the meek, for they shall inherit the earth.
> "Blessed are those who hunger and thirst for righteousness, for they shall be satisfied.
> "Blessed are the merciful, for they shall obtain mercy.
> "Blessed are the pure in heart, for they shall see God.
> "Blessed are the peacemakers, for they shall be called sons of God.
> "Blessed are those who are persecuted for righteousness' sake, for theirs is the kingdom of heaven.
> "Blessed are you when men revile you and persecute you and utter all kinds of evil against you falsely on my account. Rejoice and be glad, for your reward is great in heaven, for so men persecuted the prophets who were before you." (Matthew 5:1–12)

Here again, OSV has a resource to make this more relevant for little ones: *The Beatitudes for Children,* also by Rosemarie Gortler and Donna Piscitelli.

THE VIRTUES

For additional positive ways of thinking and behaving, your family might discuss virtues. The *Catechism of the Catholic Church* describes the virtues that Catholics (and really all Christians) should aspire to, and anchors them in the Bible. Consider:

> "Whatever is true, whatever is honorable, whatever is just, whatever is pure, whatever is lovely, whatever is gracious, if there is any excellence, if there is anything worthy of praise, think about these things" (Philippians 4:8).
>
> A virtue is an habitual and firm disposition to do the good. It allows the person not only to perform good acts, but to give the best of himself. The virtuous person tends toward the good with all his sensory and spiritual powers; he pursues the good and chooses it in concrete actions.
>
> The goal of a virtuous life is to become like God. (1803)

The *Catechism* first explains the human virtues, which are "firm attitudes, stable dispositions, habitual perfections of intellect and will that govern our actions, order our passions, and guide our conduct according to reason and faith. They make possible ease, self-mastery, and joy in leading a morally good life. The virtuous man is he who freely practices the good" (1804).

There are four primary *human* virtues that take center stage. The Bible sometimes uses other words to refer to these goals. (Yup, goals! The Beatitudes, the virtues, and the fruits of the Spirit, which we'll get to in a minute, are a perfectly valid foundation for your family's goal setting.) But they're widely known as prudence, justice, fortitude, and temperance (1804–1809).

There are also three *theological* virtues. Though you might think so at first (or was it just me?), these are not related to being a theologian; rather, they are gifts from God that detail how we relate to the Father, Son, and Holy Spirit, whereas the *human* virtues focus on how we relate to one another. The three theological virtues are faith, hope, and charity (1812–1829).

Grounding a discussion of virtues in day-to-day family life might be difficult using the passages in the *Catechism.* (They are rather scholarly.) But OSV offers an eight-page brochure called *Catholic Parent Know-How: Virtues and Discipline* by Lynne M. Lang, which can help you structure your own life around the virtues. It offers positive discipline methods for children (the old honey-versus-vinegar approach we've been talking about here) and even provides some conversation starters and a family prayer that you can use with your kids.

If you want to dive deep into the virtues along with your kiddos, check out *The Virtues for Catholic Youth*, from Catholic Sprouts. It is a twelve-week study designed for kids in grades three through eight, helping them and their parents experience each of the virtues through its contrasting vice, through the saints, through the Old and New Testaments, and through action steps.

THE GIFTS AND FRUITS OF THE SPIRIT

Finally, all of this leads us to the gifts and fruits of the Holy Spirit — here again, not just fodder for family rule-setting, but also a possible basis for some of the goals you'll be setting soon. First, the gifts:

> The moral life of Christians is sustained by the gifts of the Holy Spirit. These are permanent dispositions which make man docile in following the promptings of the Holy Spirit.
>
> The seven *gifts* of the Holy Spirit are wisdom, understanding, counsel, fortitude, knowledge, piety, and fear of the Lord. They belong in their fullness to Christ, Son of David [cf. Isaiah 11:1–2]. They complete and perfect the virtues of those who receive them. They make the faithful docile in readily obeying divine inspirations. (CCC 1830–1831)

Each of us received these gifts in baptism, and they are strengthened and confirmed in us at confirmation. In order to make them active in our lives, we need to unwrap them each day. For me, wisdom, understanding, and fortitude are three in particular that I really need to focus on every day. I'm always grateful when the Holy Spirit hears my desperate pleas and sends more my way.

The fruits of the Spirit come from these gifts. They are "perfections that the Holy Spirit forms in us as the first fruits of eternal glory" (CCC 1832). Galatians 5:22–23 says, "But the fruit of the spirit is love, joy, peace, patience, kindness, goodness, faithfulness, gentleness, self-control; against such there is no law." The tradition of the Catholic Church expands upon this list, using an ancient translation, naming twelve: charity, joy, peace, patience, kindness, goodness, generosity, gentleness, faithfulness, modesty, self-control, and chastity.

JUST TO BE CLEAR

So, the Church and the Bible offer a deep well of to-dos and not-to-dos from which you can shape your family's rules of engagement to guide this process. But just in case they still aren't immediately evident, here are some basics used by corporate teams and youth groups alike that you may want to apply to your family:

- Begin and end your get-togethers on time.
- Come prepared.
- No interrupting.
- Practice good listening.
- Pay attention to the speaker.
- Repeat what you think you heard to make sure you understand.
- If necessary, choose an object to serve as a "talking token," so that taking turns is a visible process.
- If necessary, use a timer to make sure that no one individual holds the floor too long.
- Use only loving or encouraging words.
- No "yucking" someone's "yums." It's hurtful when a person expresses a like or preference, and another replies with "Ewwwwwwww." Honor those differences.

BRAINSTORMING

Review tips one through four and make a list of things you'll need for your first family kick-off. Keep in mind your kids, your family vibe, and a means of creating structure that honors everyone. Above all, consider how to engage everyone in some team fun!

Week 1 is next. Are you excited to set out on this adventure? As you begin your family meet-ups, please remember these points:

Keep it fun: Use positive phrases, not "not" phrases. Celebrate successes often. Small ones too!

Seize the moment: Don't let life run your life. It's easier said than done, but some things may have to go. Don't let life become "someday."

Most importantly, know that you are more than equipped to do this. Simply being intentional about growing closer as a family and to God is half the battle; using the tools here, you're certain to move the needle. Now is the time. How will you change the world? This is not abstract — you've got God on your side!

"And this is the confidence which we have in him, that if we ask anything according to his will he hears us" (1 John 5:14).

WEEK 1

DATE ____________ TIME____________ PLACE ______________________________

OPENING RITUAL

Remember, parents, this is up to you and your creativity! Is it a song that you sing or listen to together? A "ready-set-go" team chant? A minute of jumping jacks to get out the wiggles? Try out some ways to make your meetings "official," and create a mood of openness and engagement.

PRAYER

Take sixty seconds to pray together. You can pray in silence, or you can recite a traditional prayer such as the Our Father or Hail Mary.

LET'S CHAT

And with that, welcome to Week 1! In one of your first official family sessions (assemblies? forums?), you're going to get to talk about everyone's favorite subject: themselves.

You're going to begin to answer the question, *So what's our family all about?* Here are some questions to help guide your discussion.

- What's the essence of your family?
- What things do you do most often or best?
- If your next-door neighbors or closest family friends were to introduce your family to a crowd at a backyard barbecue, what would they say?

Remember: Describing who you are and your purpose as a family could look *very different* from those who live next door, those in your extended family, and those in your parish. Yes, as Catholics, we share a set of beliefs. And we share a mission to love God with all our hearts, minds, bodies, and souls, and to love our neighbors as ourselves. But there are a million ways to express and achieve that.

Each member of your family is uniquely made, with gifts, talents, interests, drives, and abilities! Some are blessed with talents of outreach and friendliness; others are more quiet and inwardly focused. Some can write, some can sing, some are great business thinkers. Talking about *your* family's unique characteristics will help you to identify and shape your family's purpose in this world as God's beloved creation … a.k.a. your mission.

Author and inspirational speaker Simon Sinek talks about mission in terms of an organization's (or, we could add, a family's) *why*: "The WHY is the purpose, cause, or belief that drives every organization and every person's individual career. Why does your company exist? Why did you get out of bed this morning? And why should anyone care?"[1]

Your family's *why* — your mission — should be a natural fit. No one is going to suggest that my family's mission is to help high school students improve their career opportunities by tutoring them in math. Only two of us really understand calculus, and it's no one's favorite way to spend the day. God has created math geniuses, but he did not place them in our family.

We love to be outdoors, however, and we're all really active. Our natural abilities and our passions will lend themselves well to a purpose or cause — a mission — that shows we love God with all our hearts, minds, bodies, and souls, and we love our neighbors as ourselves. We'll just do so differently than the family whose definition of hiking is walking around the block on the sidewalk.

Pope St. John Paul II wrote at length about the mission of the family. (The following passage is helpful for parents; if you have older kids, you can read it aloud with them, too.) For younger children, the line, "Family, become what you are," is great food for thought:

> The family finds in the plan of God the Creator and Redeemer not only its identity, what it is, but also its mission, what it can and should do. The role that God calls the family to perform in history derives from what the family is; its role represents the dynamic and existential development of what it is. Each family finds within itself a summons that cannot be ignored, and that specifies both its dignity and its responsibility: family, become what you are.
>
> Accordingly, the family must go back to the "beginning" of God's creative act, if it is to attain self-knowledge and self-realization in accordance with the inner truth not only of what it is but also of what it does in history. And since in God's plan it has been established as an "intimate community of life and love," [44] the family has the mission to become more and more what it is, that is to say, a community of life and love, in an effort that will find fulfillment, as will everything created and redeemed, in the Kingdom of God. Looking at it in such a way as to reach its very roots, we must say that the essence and role of the family are in the final analysis specified by love. Hence the family has the mission to guard, reveal and communicate love, and this is a living reflection of and a real sharing in God's love for humanity and the love of Christ the Lord for the Church His bride.
>
> Every particular task of the family is an expressive and concrete actuation of that fundamental mission. We must therefore go deeper into the unique riches of the family's mission and probe its contents, which are both manifold and unified.[2]

As you can see, the idea of a "mission" for your family isn't a new one. A mission isn't just for businesses, nor is it just a trip overseas to help people. Take some time now to talk over this message from Pope St. John Paul II, and make some notes. Be sure that everyone has a turn sharing their ideas! After you've finished, make sure everyone has a copy of what you talked about, so that you can think it over in the coming week and revisit it in weeks 2 and 3, when we talk about talents, and then values and interests.

PRAYER

Dear God, "I praise you because I am fearfully and wonderfully made" (Psalm 139:14, NIV). Please help me see how the way that you created me is unique, and how I can best honor your special plan for me. Amen!

WEEK 2

DATE ____________ TIME____________ PLACE ______________________

OPENING RITUAL

Remember, parents, this is up to you and your creativity! Is it a song that you sing or listen to together? A "ready-set-go" team chant? A minute of jumping jacks to get out the wiggles? Try out some ways to make your meetings "official" and create a mood of openness and engagement.

PRAYER

Take sixty seconds to pray together. You can pray in silence, or you can recite a traditional prayer such as the Our Father or Hail Mary.

LET'S CHAT

Today we're talking about talents. Sure, they might be the kind that you display on stage at the school talent show: a great singing voice, gymnastics skills, or the ability to memorize a passage. But they might also be what you'd call personality traits: patience, a way with kids, extra finesse when managing people, a gift for seeing someone's needs — that sort of thing.

"AS EACH HAS RECEIVED A GIFT, EMPLOY IT FOR ONE ANOTHER, AS GOOD STEWARDS OF GOD'S VARIED GRACE." (1 PETER 4:10)

If you're stuck, the website helpfulprofessor.com has a list of forty-seven talents.[3] It's broken down by category, including: artistic; sporting; academic and resume; interpersonal; and personal. This could bring to light some unappreciated gifts among your team.

Identifying your talents is more than a feel-good exercise! This is how God made you, and he calls you to use those talents that he's given you to serve him. Check out 1 Peter 4:10: "As each has received a gift, employ it for one another, as good stewards of God's varied grace."

This is not time for talents to be weighed and judged. Your family is one part of God's body, with a different role to play than any other family. And the individual members of your family are different parts of a whole as well, with individual talents, skills, and abilities.

You could think of your family as the hand, and the individual members of your family as fingers on that hand. Each of you has a role to play in your family team, and your team has a role to play within the league that is God's creation.

Saint Paul writes about this:

For the body does not consist of one member but of many. If the foot should say, "Because

> I am not a hand, I do not belong to the body," that would not make it any less a part of the body. And if the ear should say, "Because I am not an eye, I do not belong to the body," that would not make it any less a part of the body. If the whole body were an eye, where would be the hearing? If the whole body were an ear, where would be the sense of smell? But as it is, God arranged the organs in the body, each one of them, as he chose. If all were a single organ, where would the body be? As it is, there are many parts, yet one body. (1 Corinthians 12:14–20)

Your kids should definitely take part in considering their individual strengths, as well as your family's. This is a fantastic opportunity to identify the beauty in differences (especially among bickering siblings) and feel personally committed to embracing and using them for good.

One very loving way to go about this is to ask each member of your family to describe the talents of another member of your family. (Why do we never take the time to tell each other these things?) The recipient might be surprised and flattered to hear the high opinion of another. The *Catechism* explains why this is so important: "The relationships within the family bring an affinity of feelings, affections and interests, arising above all from the members' respect for one another" (2206).

But also let each person speak for him or herself. You also might be surprised to hear the things on your kids' hearts.

In what ways do you think you can use your individual and family talents "as good stewards of God's varied grace"? Think about the picture that emerges when you pool all of your gifts as a team. (You could even draw a picture with little ones.) In which direction is God sending you?

You don't need to be specific yet. (That comes later!) Right now, make some notes from your discussion about talents. You might call this your "List of the Ways We're Awesome and Wonderfully Made." Post it where everyone can see it, add to it if needed, and relish the recognition of God's incredible creation.

PRAYER

Reading Matthew 5:14–16 is a great way to think about the importance of your talents:

> You are the light of the world. A city set on a hill cannot be hid. Nor do men light a lamp and put it under a bushel, but on a stand, and it gives light to all in the house. Let your light so shine before men, that they may see your good works and give glory to your Father who is in heaven.

Close your time together with a few high fives and amens — because you are an awesome light!

WEEK 3

DATE ____________ TIME____________ PLACE ______________________

OPENING RITUAL

Remember, parents, this is up to you and your creativity! Is it a song that you sing or listen to together? A "ready-set-go" team chant? A minute of jumping jacks to get out the wiggles? Try out some ways to make your meetings "official" and create a mood of openness and engagement.

PRAYER

Take sixty seconds to pray together. You can pray in silence, or you can recite a traditional prayer such as the Our Father or Hail Mary.

LET'S CHAT

What kinds of things are important to your family? What are your passions? Your priorities? What rules do you and your family live by?

This week we're talking about values and interests. Values are "big." They are those ideas and rules that tell you what's most important in life, especially when you have to make a choice. Interests are more specific. They are the activities that you enjoy doing and the topics that hold your interest.

Of course, each member of your family likely has different interests. You may even have different values … or at least different top-ten-values lists. Identifying these will help shape your mission. And they might reveal some things about one another that you never even knew! Grab some popcorn, because this is like making the documentary of your family and yourselves.

Let's start with values. If you're like me, it helps to have a list to choose from. Russ Harris, a doctor who became an author and a trainer in Acceptance and Commitment Therapy, published a book called *The Confidence Gap*. Along with it, he created a worksheet listing lots of values. You can find that within the free resources at thehappinesstrap.com.[4]

I like what he says at the start of that worksheet, because it helps distinguish values from virtues or interests: "Values are your heart's deepest desires for how you want to behave as a human being. Values are not about what you want to get or achieve; they are about how you want to behave or act on an ongoing basis."

Take some time to talk about what values are important to each of you. Make a list, and see where there's overlap.

Values can be pretty vague for little ones, so consider hanging your list somewhere visible, and take a tip from behavioral science expert Angela Duckworth:[5] Spend the next week linking words to actions. When your child asks questions or looks something up, point out that she is curious. When your child reaches out to include a sibling or friend, congratulate him for being kind and inclusive. Name these values as you see them in action.

Interests are a little bit simpler to articulate. Dinosaurs, Barbies, books, soccer ... you can likely make a quick list for each child. But be sure to ask them, too; here again, you might learn something that you didn't know about your child's inner life. And share your own interests, too. Kids often fail to imagine their parents as anything but parents; allow them to get to know you as people.

Keep track of these values and interests just as you did your talents from last week. This is all going to come together next week, when you write your mission statement.

FOOD FOR THOUGHT

If you've applied for a position with a new employer, or you work in human relations, you're probably familiar with the idea of corporate culture. This is the idea that each firm or company has its own unique personality.

Some workplaces are very formal — people dress nicely; no one shares much personal small talk; employees stick to their roles. Some are very casual — everyone pitches in on a project when a deadline nears; the staff feels like an extended family; and T-shirts are a valid wardrobe choice for the Monday morning meeting.

Because your family is operating as a microcosm of a team, a business, and — most importantly — as a domestic church, think for a little bit about your "corporate culture." Are you formal or casual? Do you operate in silos, or is cross-departmental communication strong? Is there a lot of buy-in and participation? Do members feel valued? What's turnover like? Not that anyone is quitting your family, but are any of you champing at the bit for the day when the kids grow up and move out, or do you enjoy your time under one roof?

No family operates smoothly all the time. No company or team or church always functions well. But successful ones pay attention to the culture. And when they see an issue, they actively address it.

One way to assess the culture in your family is to host a company-wide survey. You don't have to print sheets with multiple-choice answers that you fill out with No. 2 pencils. Just choose a few questions for discussion that will elicit more detailed responses than "fine." Examples include:[6]

- What does it take to be successful in our family?
- If there is one roadblock between the family's ideal culture and the way it really is, what is it?
- Which of the family's values speaks to you the most?
- Talk about a time when you were especially proud to be associated with this family.

The "corporate culture" of your household informs your family identity. And your family identity, if it's a positive one, is what your kids will cherish and carry forward, both into their engagement with the world and the formation of their own family. It's fully worth examining for a lifetime of closeness with one another.

PRAYER

Dear Holy Spirit, please fill us with the confidence and wisdom to live our faith to the best of our abilities and with real enthusiasm, embracing our roles to teach one another and support our team. We're grateful for your guidance and courage in our words and actions. Amen!

WEEK 4

DATE ____________ TIME____________ PLACE ______________________

OPENING RITUAL

Remember, parents, this is up to you and your creativity! Is it a song that you sing or listen to together? A "ready-set-go" team chant? A minute of jumping jacks to get out the wiggles? Try out some ways to make your meetings "official" and create a mood of openness and engagement.

PRAYER

Take sixty seconds to pray together. You can pray in silence, or you can recite a traditional prayer such as the Our Father or Hail Mary.

LET'S CHAT

This week, you're going to write your family's mission statement. All those notes from the last three weeks are going to come together now!

Using the notes that you made about your talents, values, and interests, you'll craft a few sentences that describe:

- Who you are
- What you do
- For whom you do it
- What you value
- Your purpose

Within this framework, be creative for your family. Maybe you're a family of talented amateur chefs who love to cook, and you value contribution and connection. Your purpose is to make a positive difference for the lonely through meals that bring people together.

> ***IT CAN BE REALLY AFFIRMING FOR YOUR FAMILY TO REALIZE EXACTLY WHAT KIND OF GREATNESS YOU CAN OFFER TO THE WORLD.***

This exercise isn't just a chore; it can be really affirming for your family to realize exactly what kind of greatness you can offer to the world. Talk it through and celebrate your family — bond over your amazing, God-given talents!

Be sure you let everyone speak. No idea is wrong. And be sure to capture the popcorn thinking. You could do this with a whiteboard, or designate a note-taker, or use a recording app such as Otter, which lets everyone participate without having to write at the same time.

Also helpful: Provide note paper and pencils for everyone. This minimizes interruptions by those who are sure they'll forget their idea if they don't spit it out *right now*, even if someone else is already talking. (Refer back to the tips in chapter 4 for more suggestions on managing your family meetings.)

Think about these questions and answer as many as you can. Don't worry about perfect answers or complete sentences. You can clean all of this up later. And don't give this so much weight that it overwhelms you; your family will change over the years, so your mission may morph, too. Just get started:

- Who are we?
- What makes our family special, different, and unique?
- What do we do best as a family?
- What are we really proud of as a family?
- What are our family's skills, strengths, experiences, and gifts — our talents?
- What's most important to our family? What do we stand for and believe in? What are our values?
- What are we most passionate about? What are our interests?
- How do we fit into our parish/our neighborhood/our community/the world?
- How can we use all of our special talents, values, and interests to serve our parish/our neighborhood/our community/the world?

____

____

____

____

____

____

____

____

____

____

Be sure to use language that's age appropriate. Ditch the formal statements for little children. Are you good singers? Do you value kindness? Consider for whom you might make music (one another, extended family members, the neighbor, nursing home residents) to share some extra kindness. Toddlers and preschoolers love to sing, so kindly make some noise!

Write a rough draft. Tweak it if you need to. And once you have some good answers, give one another high-fives, then put it all away and let it rest for at least a few days. This gives everyone time to think of other responses they may have forgotten in the moment, and to gain some perspective on the things they did share.

In closing, take a moment to honor the ways in which we're all different but wonderfully made by reading or singing "This Little Light of Mine." If you need a refresher on the lyrics, want to connect it to relevant Bible verses, or listen to a jazzy, bluesy performance, check out "This Little Light of Mine" on Godtube.com.

PRAYER

Dear Jesus, it's sometimes really hard to talk about ourselves and how great we are. But identifying our talents is actually the first step toward using the gifts that you gave us. So, help us remember: "Let your light so shine before men, that they may see your good works and give glory to your Father who is in heaven" (Matthew 5:16). Amen.

WEEK 5

DATE ____________ TIME ____________ PLACE ______________________________

OPENING RITUAL

WAIT! Before you just slide into your usual routine, why not share a high-five all around? You've been at this for a month now. Greet your kids with some posters or balloons or a special snack. It's time to celebrate the effort that you've put in and the progress that you've made!

PRAYER

Take sixty seconds to pray together. You can pray in silence, or you can recite a traditional prayer such as the Our Father or Hail Mary.

LET'S CHAT

This week, let's begin the habit of a weekly mission statement review. How you want to do that is up to you and your creativity! You could challenge older kids to recite it from memory. Or take a minute to allow each person to sketch an image of your family living out your mission. Set it to music with some kind of backbeat. The sky's the limit!

OUR MISSION STATEMENT

____

____

____

____

____

Talk about displaying your mission somewhere where everyone can see it and be inspired by it each and every day. Some ideas:

- Print a custom banner.

- Write it out with refrigerator magnets.
- Hang a chalkboard, and assign a different family member each week to rewrite and decorate your mission statement.
- Send out a Friday morning text message with your mission statement to each member of your family.
- Jot it down on a sticky note and place it on the TV remote, or the cookie jar, or the coffee pot — find a new spot each week.
- Write it on a bunch of slips of paper, put them in plastic Easter eggs, and stash one in a different hiding spot every Sunday. The one who finds it gets to speak first at your family get-together.

Is your mission statement working for everyone? If not, now's the time to tweak it. Your vision and goals will unfold from your mission statement, so while you can always scratch it and start over, it's easier to maintain momentum if you can keep this foundation consistent during the coming year and reevaluate next year.

Before we move on to your family's vision statement, I'd like to offer one final succinct review of mission versus vision, borrowing from the marketing industry in which I work.

In "What Is a Brand Mission and How to Define It," business-to-business content strategist Sarah Aboulhosn writes, "The mission describes what your brand aims to achieve and how you will achieve it. The vision statement defines where you want those achievements to lead in the future."[7]

Substitute "family" for "brand" here, and keep in mind that we will address "how you will achieve it" with your goals. If you have a good handle on your family's unique purpose in this world, then you're ready to talk about how you're going to change the world.

As you go, know that you're part of an exciting tradition. Consider this fun fact: The word "Mass" comes from the Latin word "Missa." At one time, the people were dismissed with the words *Ite, missa est* (meaning "Go, she — meaning you, the Church — has been sent"). The word "Missa" is related to the word "missio," the root of the English word "mission." The liturgy does not simply come to an end. Those assembled are sent forth to bring the fruits of the Eucharist to the world.[8]

PRAYER

Take a moment to close with a prayer:

> Dear Father in heaven, help us see people the way that you see people: as one family of people united by your love for us and our longing for you. May we offer everyone the dignity with which you've created us. Thank you for building a world so full of beautiful diversity! Amen.

WEEK 6

DATE ____________ TIME____________ PLACE ______________________________

OPENING RITUAL

Remember, parents, this is up to you and your creativity! Is it a song that you sing or listen to together? A "ready-set-go" team chant? A minute of jumping jacks to get out the wiggles? Try out some ways to make your meetings "official" and create a mood of openness and engagement.

PRAYER

Take sixty seconds to pray together. You can pray in silence, or you can recite a traditional prayer such as the Our Father or Hail Mary.

MISSION REVIEW

Ask someone to recite, write, or sing your family's mission statement.

LET'S CHAT

I've always loved the song "Change the World," especially as recorded by Babyface in 1997. I think it helps that it came out at the same time my daughter was born; we listened to it on repeat, and my love *was* (is!) really something good.

The song also radiates the optimism that a vision statement requires. A vision statement is aspirational. Lofty. It's dreaming big. It's the change you wish to create in the world as a result of living out your mission and reaching your goals. It's becoming all that you were intended to be.

This week is the time for a family conversation about how each of you, as well as the members of your community and the world as a whole, will be better because of your teamwork in living out your mission.

PERHAPS YOU THINK THAT CHANGING THE WORLD IS BEYOND YOUR FAMILY. BUT KEEP IN MIND THAT WE'RE CALLED TO GO FORTH, AND THAT WITH GOD, WE'RE CAPABLE OF ANYTHING.

It's important to spend time thinking about this; otherwise, you could just spend your time dealing with whatever comes your way. At FranklinCovey.com, "Habit 2: Begin with the End in Mind" explains this: "If you don't make a conscious effort to visualize who you are and what you want in life, then you empower other people and circumstances to shape you and your life by default." Perhaps you think that changing the world is beyond your family. But keep in mind that we're called to go forth, and that with God, we're capable of anything.

So, talk it over with your kids. Ask little ones to use their imaginations — what does the world look like because they're living the way Jesus wants them to and letting their little light shine? Ask older kids how they think the world will be better off because your family is in it. How does living out your purpose make the world a better place?

And pray. Ask God what he wants the world to look like with you in it. Be sure to take time to listen!

It might be helpful to come up with a list of inspirational phrases to kick-start your vision-writing process. (The Beatitudes, the virtues, and the fruits of the Spirit are great resources for ideas.) Here are a few aspirational ideas to get the creative juices flowing:

- Our community will be more peaceful.
- People who meet us will experience exceptional kindness.
- God's creation will reflect our love.
- People who are down on their luck will feel encouraged.

If your kids are older, you could take some quiet time to engage in "future journaling," a concept described by Kaki Okumura, author of a Japanese wellness blog, in "Why You Should Write Notes to Your Future Self."[9] She suggests: "Imagine yourself at this future moment and what the ideal version of you would look like. How did you move past this challenge you're struggling with now?"

As you imagine how your family might look a year from now, allow each person to write a letter to him- or herself, or to the family as a whole, articulating what you hope things will look like (without getting bogged down in how you got there).

As you brainstorm your family vision, you can designate a person to write the ideas on a whiteboard. Or, if you have some family members who typically control the conversation and others who usually remain silent, ask everyone to write a few words on paper and turn in all the slips.

Remember at this point to keep it brief and abstract. A vision statement doesn't include the how-to — you'll get to that in your goals. Here, you're just dreaming about what heaven on earth might actually look like.

You may describe in your vision who will be impacted by your teamwork. Is it your family? Your neighborhood? Your city? The planet? Some combination of these? The scope can grow as your family grows up, but be careful not to squash tiny ones' giant aspirations. Belief and effort, unencumbered by potentially unnecessary rules and realities, can often be powerful forces.

Don't feel as if you have to rush to a conclusion. Take time. Pray. Brainstorm. Reach. Don't be afraid to fail. Don't narrow your thinking. Ask, "What if? Why not?" After all, you're working with God!

OUR VISION STATEMENT

____

____

____

____

____

____

____

____

Let your family think on your ideas over the coming week.

PRAYER

End your time this week by prayerfully reading this Scripture passage:

> But Jesus looked at them and said to them, "With men, this is impossible, but with God all things are possible." (Matthew 19:26)

WEEK 7

DATE ____________ TIME____________ PLACE ________________________

OPENING RITUAL

Remember, parents, this is up to you and your creativity! Is it a song that you sing or listen to together? A "ready-set-go" team chant? A minute of jumping jacks to get out the wiggles? Try out some ways to make your meetings "official" and create a mood of openness and engagement.

> **PRAYER**
>
> Take sixty seconds to pray together. You can pray in silence, or you can recite a traditional prayer such as the Our Father or Hail Mary.

MISSION REVIEW

Ask someone to recite, write, or sing your family's mission statement.

LET'S CHAT

How can you harness a hope? Draw a dream? Write a wish? This week we're going to put big ideas on paper. It's time to write your family's vision statement.

Business banking company Brex provides some questions that can help you incorporate the key elements of a vision statement. (See www.brex.com/blog/vision-statement-examples/.) I've tweaked them for families:

- What can we achieve?
- What problem does our family intend to solve?
- What are the changes we believe our family can make for individuals? For our community? For the world?
- How will things be different if our vision is realized?
- What phrases or keywords describe the type of family and outcome we want?

This doesn't have to be an elaborate paragraph. One sentence will do — or even a part of a sentence! Take this statement from Catholic Relief Services, for example:

> "Demonstrated through measurable outcomes, our actions must be effective in alleviating human suffering, removing root causes and empowering people to achieve their full potential."

Can you see right away what parts of this are visionary? "Alleviating human suffering" and "empowering people to achieve their full potential" are two statements that describe how they want the world to be different as a result of their work.

Take a minute to reread your mission as a family. Then read the vision statement that you drafted last week. Do they go together? Does your vision make logical sense based on your mission — is it specifically related to your mission (which came from your talents, values, and interests)?

Your vision is going to serve as a little if/then test for the coming year — and the coming weeks, when you write your goals. When your family has to make a decision about how you spend your time, your money, your energy, or other resources, you can ask:

- If we do x, then are we closer to achieving our vision?
- Or, if we don't do x, then are we closer to achieving our vision?

We talked about this before, but it bears gentle repeating: If you don't set priorities for how you spend your time, then life and general busyness will. I *completely* understand that many things aren't a matter of choice. You probably have to work — maybe two jobs. You have to shop for groceries, clean the house, make meals. You have to get everyone to the dentist. You likely have very little time over which you have authority.

But you can make time for your priorities by carving them out first. Sometimes, it might be just twenty minutes. And then you can filter all other decisions through that priority: Does this activity meet the test of bringing us closer to achieving our vision? Are there other things in our lives that we need to cut, so that we still have room for the steps that will lead to our vision? And if this activity doesn't directly further that vision (which is fine — not everything will), can it at least be molded around that sacred vision and leave space for it?

When you set goals (next week), the same kinds of questions will come into play. Goals are the concrete actions — the things that you do — to fulfill your purpose and move you toward your vision.

Your vision will act as your guiding light. And it's derived from your mission: You've established who you are, what's important to you, what you're good at, and your purpose in your community and the world. Now, what is the result of your presence, your strengths, and your passion? How are you going to change the world?

It might take some courage, but remember who is on your side.

PRAYER

End your family get-together this week by prayerfully reading this Scripture passage:

> Be strong and of good courage, do not fear or be in dread of them: for it is the LORD your God who goes with you; he will not fail you or forsake you. (Deuteronomy 31:6)

WEEK 8

DATE ____________ TIME____________ PLACE ______________________________

OPENING RITUAL

Remember, parents, this is up to you and your creativity! Is it a song that you sing or listen to together? A "ready-set-go" team chant? A minute of jumping jacks to get out the wiggles? Try out some ways to make your meetings "official" and create a mood of openness and engagement.

PRAYER

Take sixty seconds to pray together. You can pray in silence, or you can recite a traditional prayer such as the Our Father or Hail Mary.

MISSION REVIEW

Ask someone to recite, write, or sing your family's mission statement.

This week, take a minute to read your vision together, after you read your mission statement. It is that shining star that will inspire and lead you when things seem to go off track.

LET'S CHAT

Are you excited yet?

We're nearly finished with the planning and almost to the doing. Now's the time to develop goals out of all this big-picture thinking. This is where the rubber meets the road. And as such, this is where things can go wonderfully, or wildly, off track. Consider this time spent on goal setting an investment in helping your family not only to embrace this entire endeavor, but also to thrive throughout.

You now know your talents, your purpose — your mission. You now know what effect your mission will have on the world — your vision. What, exactly, are you going to do to live out your mission and achieve your vision?

This is where goals come in. And as someone who has written a lot about New Year's fitness resolutions, I can assure you that some goals are more effective than others. Next week, we're going to talk about SMART goals. Once you've set your family's goals and go forward with the learning and doing, you'll find a bit of encouragement each week to help you develop habits that support your goals, reevaluate your goals, and stay on track with your goals.

This week, just take some time to brainstorm. Get out your handy dandy notebook, or your whiteboard or recording app, and talk it over.

- What kinds of activities or changes in your lives fit with your mission and look like a staircase to your vision?

- What kinds of things might get in the way?
- What are some easy things to do or change? What things will be hard to do or change?
- If you picture yourselves doing these things, how do you feel?

Actual pictures are great! Your little ones can draw pictures, or cut pictures from a magazine and make a collage.

List a few actual things that you want to do or change. Don't get hung up in the details yet — that's next week.

____

____

____

____

____

____

____

____

End your time this week by reading this passage from the Epistle of James:

> What does it profit, my brethren, if a man says he has faith but has not works? Can his faith save him? If a brother or sister is ill-clad and in lack of daily food, and one of you says to them, "Go in peace, be warmed and filled," without giving them the things needed for the body, what does it profit? So faith by itself, if it has no works, is dead.
>
> But some one will say, "You have faith and I have works." Show me your faith apart from your works, and I by my works will show you my faith. You believe that God is one; you do well. Even the demons believe — and shudder. Do you want to be shown, you

BUT SOME ONE WILL SAY, "YOU HAVE FAITH AND I HAVE WORKS." SHOW ME YOUR FAITH APART FROM YOUR WORKS, AND I BY MY WORKS WILL SHOW YOU MY FAITH." (JAMES 2:18)

> foolish fellow, that faith apart from works is barren? Was not Abraham our father justified by works, when he offered his son Isaac upon the altar? You see that faith was active along with his works, and faith was completed by works, and the Scripture was fulfilled which says, "Abraham believed God, and it was reckoned to him as righteousness"; and he was called the friend of God. You see that a man is justified by works and not by faith alone. For as the body apart from the spirit is dead, so faith apart from works is dead. (James 2:14–24, 26)

Saint James shows how a vision — "go in peace, be warmed and filled" — requires someone to actually set and meet some goals — "giving them the things needed for the body." You and your family are going to be doing the works!

PRAYER

Dear Jesus, thank you for your amazing example of how to take action and show our faith with our works. Amen.

WEEK 9

DATE ____________ TIME_____________ PLACE ________________________________

OPENING RITUAL

Remember, parents, this is up to you and your creativity! Is it a song that you sing or listen to together? A "ready-set-go" team chant? A minute of jumping jacks to get out the wiggles? Try out some ways to make your meetings "official" and create a mood of openness and engagement.

> ## PRAYER
> Take sixty seconds to pray together. You can pray in silence, or you can recite a traditional prayer such as the Our Father or Hail Mary.

MISSION REVIEW

Ask someone to recite, write, or sing your family's mission statement.

VISION REVIEW

Read your vision statement aloud.

LET'S CHAT

You may have heard of SMART goals: Specific, Measurable, Attainable, Relevant, and Time-bound. Yes, you're very smart to set these goals! In this case, however, SMART is an acronym for goals that are more likely to be successful. Ask yourself with every goal that you set:

What, specifically, do we want to achieve? Don't use a blanket statement, such as "To be a better Catholic family." Who can really tell me exactly what that means?

Instead, be precise; here, you might narrow down that broad suggestion to something along the lines of "To serve the people in our community as described in Matthew 25:34–36." (And this will call for goals within goals, as we'll discuss shortly.)

Can we measure our progress? "More" and "better" are vague. How do you track change? A statement such as "At least 50 percent more often than we did in the past six months" is measurable.

Is this attainable? Please, please, PLEASE don't set yourselves up for failure. The worst thing you can do is go hard out of the gate and then feel discouraged just three months in. Err on the side of goals that are way too easy! Then celebrate your wins. You can always recalibrate after six months and do more, if you have the capacity.

Is this relevant? Don't make a long list of to-dos that don't actually move you toward your vision. Let that be your guiding light. Sure, you could have the prettiest Advent calendar west of the Mississippi, but if your vision was to help eliminate suffering in your community, then tie your goals to feeding the hungry or something equally community oriented.

At what point in time will we assess our results? Ideally, your mission and vision statements will serve you for a year. But I'd encourage you to check in on your goals far more often than that. Do a first round of assessments three months in. This lets everyone get into the swing of things, but allows you to shift gears if it just isn't working. Maybe you need to add or subtract other things in your life to achieve your goals. Maybe your goals are too lofty or too easy. Maybe you need reminders, or you need different tactics to achieve those goals. Don't be afraid to redo your goal setting at that point and give yourselves a new time frame.

And keep in mind this one really important tactic of treadmill users everywhere: To be truly successful, you'll need to identify trackable habits to help you meet your bigger goals.

What does this mean? Here's an easy-to-understand example from my fitness-writing experience. Marcia, a nurse, has made it her mission to bring healing and hope to the sick and hurting through her work at the local hospital. Her vision is healthier, happier patients and colleagues in her community.

So, Marcia decides on January 1 that one of her goals is to lose thirty pounds by the end of the year. This will allow her to be a more energetic nurse and a good example for her patients and colleagues. She'll also gain empathy and understanding for those struggling to implement healthy habits. This goal is:

- Specific: She will lose weight.
- Measurable: She will lose 30 pounds.
- Attainable: This is enough time to lose that much weight safely, and she will not be underweight after she reaches this goal.
- Relevant: Losing weight will inspire her patients, help her do her job better, and teach her about weight loss.
- Time-bound: She will achieve this goal by the end of the year.

See how that works? Try one now with your family. Set a goal and fill in the blanks to make sure it's a SMART one.

- Specific: ______________________________

  ____
- Measurable: ______________________________

  ____
- Attainable: ______________________________

  ____

- Relevant: ____

  ____

- Time-bound: ____

  ____

High five! You're on your way. But there's one more step: establishing habits. Marcia will fail miserably unless she identifies trackable habits that help her reach this goal to lose weight. For example:

- She needs to determine how often she will exercise, and when, and where.
- She needs to decide how she will change up her eating habits.
- She may need to create new ways to socialize — perhaps she's going to stop getting a sugar-laden mocha with her friend four days a week, and slowly transition to walks with her friend instead.

Without ever-more-specific micro goals, or habits, Marcia will never find her way to the big one. She needs to break down her progress into steps that will keep her on track. This could be exhausting, right? That's why I suggest focusing on just one larger goal for starters. Don't spread yourselves too thin.

For example: If your **mission** is to serve the people of your community as described in Matthew 25:34–36, so that you can achieve your **vision** of less suffering in your community, then you might start with the **goal** of "physically and financially supporting [name of organization in your city that ministers to the poor with food and clothing]." Then you might outline new **habits** that include volunteering your time to that organization (when?), or donating money (how much?), raising awareness (in what ways?), researching the issue in your city (schedule it), encouraging the staff (with what?), praying for the staff and those whom they serve (when?) … there are abundant ways to fill your year with trackable actions under the umbrella of a single larger goal.

Remember your family's talents and strengths here. Aim for going deep rather than broad. Take some time now to break down your family's goal into specific habits. (You might need to get out calendars!)

OUR HABITS

Dr. Art Markman, a professor of psychology and marketing at the University of Texas at Austin and the author of *Smart Change: Five Tools to Create Sustainable Habits in Yourself and Others*, identifies one ingenious aspect of building habits and creating change that I'd guess many of us overlook: managing our environments. This is the idea that you set yourself up for success by surrounding yourself with the tools and reminders you'll need to achieve your goals.

Having written about fitness for many years, I can make a long list of techniques for managing one's environment that help further health goals. For example:

- Stash a yoga mat beside your nightstand to encourage morning stretching.
- Pack your gym bag every evening after dinner and stick it in your car — preferably on the passenger seat, where you'll see it the next day after work.
- Keep socks and tennis shoes in your car so you can grab a walk whenever you find some spare time in your day — maybe waiting for soccer practice to wrap up.
- Create a playlist of favorite songs, or download a digital book or show, and only allow yourself to enjoy it while you're exercising.

I could go on. (Some days it's hard for me to get to the gym, too!) But the idea is perfectly applicable to increasing your family's progress toward your goals. Consider this:

- Want to pray more? Stash a prayer book or Bible in the car and ask your children to read it to you while you're driving, or find an app with Catholic prayers, music, or

Scripture that you can listen to.

- Want to volunteer more? Print out a calendar of opportunities and hang it in your kitchen next to your family calendar.
- Want to spend more time actively engaged with your family? Set an alarm on your phone for a specific time each day when you chat or just hug. If your kids are older, you can use a meeting-planning function such as Google Calendar to bring everyone together. Make it a recurring event!

Be creative. You can go well beyond motivational posters. (Though if motivational posters are your thing, then by all means!) Consider the spaces you already inhabit, and then place reminders and tools conspicuously to create a supportive environment.

Fr. George McKenna, the longtime, beloved chaplain at Chicago's Midway Airport, recounts a tip he gave in a sermon that stuck with one of his parishioners for decades: Before you go to sleep, put your shoes under your bed. The next morning, you'll have to get on your knees to fish them out, and you'll remember to pray. This depends, of course, on knowing which shoes you want to wear before the mad chaos of morning … which can be another challenge with kiddos. Maybe you put this plan into action and kill two birds with one stone! Find more fast wisdom from Father McKenna in *I'll Only Speak for 3 Minutes, Vol. 3* (VCA Publishing, 2000).

PRAYER

Close with this encouraging Bible verse:

> But you, take courage! Do not let your hands be weak, for your work shall be rewarded. (2 Chronicles 15:7)

WEEK 10

DATE ____________ TIME____________ PLACE ______________________________

OPENING RITUAL

Remember, parents, this is up to you and your creativity! Is it a song that you sing or listen to together? A "ready-set-go" team chant? A minute of jumping jacks to get out the wiggles? Try out some ways to make your meetings "official" and create a mood of openness and engagement.

PRAYER

Take sixty seconds to pray together. You can pray in silence, or you can recite a traditional prayer such as the Our Father or Hail Mary.

MISSION REVIEW

Ask someone to recite, write, or sing your family's mission statement.

VISION REVIEW

Read your vision statement aloud.

GOAL REVIEW

This is an open discussion that should be free of shame and full of humility from both kids and adults. You're working as a *team*. And perfection is impossible! The principles in chapter 4 really come into play at this point.

- What goal(s) are you working toward? ______________________________

  ____

- Does it still sound reasonable? ______________________________

  ____

- What systems or habits did you put into place to help you make progress?

  ____

- How did it go in this first week?______________________________

____

- What things got in the way of progress this week? What things helped?

____

- Do you need prompts or reminders? If so, how and where? ____________

____

- What things do you want to celebrate about the process this week? ________

____

- Do you need to change your habits? Do you need to change your goal(s)?

____

- How can you support one another better next week? ______________

____

Your family has been doing a lot of work! You've spent quite a bit of time thinking very hard about who you are, your talents, your values and interests, and your goals. You've even listed some new habits that you're going to be starting soon.

Take a minute to talk about those habits. Did you think of anything else since last week? Are there any that might not be realistic? What do you need to be able to change your habits and reach your goals? Be honest with yourselves.

As a family, talk about what goal or goals allow you to live out your mission and achieve your vision. Use the SMART checklist for your broader goal as well as those trackable habits that will help you get there.

And if you find after three months that you need smaller or bigger goals, fewer or more or different habits, that's OK. We're going to check in with a weekly goal review during this learning process. Keep in mind that ultimately, this is about growing closer to one another, your faith, and God.

GOAL ____

Is it specific? ______________________________________

Is it measurable? ________________________________

Is it attainable? ________________________________

Is it relevant? ________________________________

Is it time-bound? ________________________________

Habit 1 ________________________________

Who is involved? ________________________________

When will we do this? ________________________________

Where will we do this? ________________________________

How often will we do this? ________________________________

What do we need? ________________________________

What needs to change? ________________________________

Here are some prompts to help you think through your goals:

- This might be a challenge …
- This could expand …
- We'll need to include these people …
- We need to look up …

Keep in mind your mission: What do you care about? What are your family's strengths? Why are you doing this? For what were you wonderfully and uniquely made?

Keep in mind your vision: How do you want things to look when you're successful? How will your lives look one year from now? How will the world change because you're trying this?

Use your filter: As events, commitments, and invitations arise, determine whether they bring you closer to your vision, or represent a detour.

Keep your goals specific: You don't have to do it all this year … or even in this lifetime.

Plan for challenges: What are some obstacles, and how will you overcome them? What are some time wasters?

Establish support: Create visual reminders of goals and successes. Support one another generously. Enlist or join people in your community doing the same things!

Reassess: Give yourselves time to establish habits, but check in. If it isn't working, pivot.

As your family implements new habits, you might find it hard to make them stick. If so, see what existing habits you can tack new habits onto. "One of the best ways to develop a new habit is to tie it to an existing one," writes health and science writer Dr. Dana G. Smith in "Habits Are the New Resolutions."[10]

PLAN FOR CHALLENGES: WHAT ARE SOME OBSTACLES, AND HOW WILL YOU OVERCOME THEM? WHAT ARE SOME TIME WASTERS?

So, think about your current habits. Does your family have an after-dinner ice cream routine? Are you also trying to read the Bible together? Place a Bible next to the drawer with the ice cream scoop. (And invite me to dinner, OK?) Do you sit down together in the evening and grab the remote? Are you trying to spend time each day listening to God? Place a timer next to the remote and spend two minutes praying together before you turn on a show.

I've grown legs of steel by tying my tooth-brushing habit to a leg-lifts and calf-raises routine. In fact, both have grown so mindless that I've started reading a daily meditation while I brush and lift. I can attest that this practice of tacking on habits works … as long as you can keep your balance.

PRAYER

Close your time this week by prayerfully reading this Scripture passage: "Many are the plans in the mind of a man, but it is the purpose of the Lord that will be established" (Proverbs 19:21). Check in and see: Do the plans of the man, or woman, or kids in your family align with God's purpose? Ask the Holy Spirit to keep you on track.

Talk about what you think this Bible verse means. (Of course, "man" can mean "woman" or "kid" as well.) Do you think your plans are aligned with God's purpose?

WEEK 11

DATE ____________ TIME____________ PLACE ______________________________

OPENING RITUAL

Remember, parents, this is up to you and your creativity! Is it a song that you sing or listen to together? A "ready-set-go" team chant? A minute of jumping jacks to get out the wiggles? Try out some ways to make your meetings "official" and create a mood of openness and engagement.

PRAYER

Take sixty seconds to pray together. You can pray in silence, or you can recite a traditional prayer such as the Our Father or Hail Mary.

MISSION REVIEW

Ask someone to recite, write, or sing your family's mission statement.

VISION REVIEW

Read your vision statement aloud.

GOAL REVIEW

List your family's goals and habits.

LET'S CHAT

Now that you've nailed down some really SMART, solid goals and habits, discuss ways to keep them at the forefront of your daily life. Do you need written reminders? An alarm on your phone? Do you need to tie a new habit to an old one to help you remember?

Look at your family calendar and talk about how to filter things through the lens of mission, vision, and goals, such as kids' activities or family vacations. How do you stay on track when you have a full day at the soccer field and a birthday party to attend that evening?

Talk about how to measure growth and the potential need to readjust. Are you using stickers on charts? Marbles in a jar? Downloading a habit-tracking app?

This week, you should also discuss one other very important part of goal setting: celebrating your achievements! This isn't extra — you should build this into your plan.

Think carefully about how each member of your family is motivated. Does one love a great big pizza with the whole family, followed by game night? Does one thrive on daily high-fives and a written love letter of praise? Does one long for a quiet day with no to-do list and the opportunity to recharge? Be sure you include something for all to anticipate and relish. This kind of motivation is important, and we even find it in the Bible: The Letter to the Hebrews urges us, "And let us consider how to stir up one another to love and good works" (10:24).

Celebrate often. Talk about it and honor the effort daily. Check in weekly. Evaluate monthly. Positive reinforcement is the secret sauce — for grown-ups as well!

Keep in mind, too, that you're a team. This isn't the time to scrutinize the kids the way you might when discussing their homework or chore list. You're all in this together, and a win for one is a win for everyone. A challenge for one is an opportunity for everyone to work together to overcome it. Demonstrate respect for your children's beautiful hearts, clever ideas, and honest attempts.

Setting goals can be a really tricky process. Achieving them — or striving to achieve them as a family without getting discouraged or losing momentum — can be even harder. Remember that this process is to be fun, encouraging, and life-giving. It's time to build up and support one another, and to grow as a team. Remember, being a part of God's family and our own family is *joyful*. Joyful!

So, round up your team, put in place the tools you'll need to build your habits and achieve your goals, and keep your mission and vision in mind.

PRAYER

"For God so loved the world that he gave his only-begotten Son, that whoever believes in him should not perish but have eternal life" (John 3:16). Thank you, God, for a love that's bigger than everything! Amen.

WEEK 12

DATE ____________ TIME____________ PLACE ______________________________

This week, rather than reviewing your mission, vision, and goals, take this time to celebrate! You've been working together toward this cause for almost a quarter of a year. Way to go!

Use this time to tell one another about the things you've learned about each other in the past three months. Think about ways you've caught one another being good, doing something special, or putting in extra effort. Share success stories. Honor the beautiful hearts of your family members.

Enjoy some of the best parts of your kickoff soiree. Was there an activity, some music, or some food that everyone loved? Revisit chapter 4, tip 3, if you need a refresher. Recapture that energy, and turn family favorites into traditions.

ENCOURAGEMENT

In July 2016, Pope Francis tweeted, "True joy which is experienced in the family is not something random and fortuitous, but normal and ongoing." By now, you've likely experienced the joy of coming together as a team, a domestic church, and some of your efforts have probably become normal and ongoing.

Look back at your family life before you started this process, and consider how it's changed in just three months. Imagine how much greater your joy will be as your relationships with God and one another continue to grow!

Next week, you'll notice a new format that'll stick for the rest of the year. You will begin with the usual review, but then learn a little something about the Catholic Church, and read some encouragement and wisdom from experts and successful people about productivity, helpful habits, mindset, and planning to help you in your grand adventure. Finally, you'll close with a prayer.

"TRUE JOY WHICH IS EXPERIENCED IN THE FAMILY IS NOT SOMETHING RANDOM AND FORTUITOUS, BUT NORMAL AND ONGOING."
— POPE FRANCIS

After every family soiree, follow up with a short summary of what was said and decided, plus some notes for next time. You can assign the task of notetaking to one family member, or take turns. Even if your kiddos are small, a single word plus a home-made illustration of the topic is helpful to keep everyone on track. This isn't City Council, after all. Add a favorite encouraging quote. Don't spend a ton of time on it, but do make it whimsy and fun.

This will help keep you all literally on the same page!

PRAYER

This blessing (benediction) is a fantastic prayer for people who are getting ready to go and do big things. It's a tall order, but keep in mind with whom you're working (God!). It offers challenge, but it also provides inspiration. See how your family's mission fits somewhere in here. After you've prayed the prayer together, you might want to use a dictionary or thesaurus to help you find synonyms for the bigger words that will better resonate with younger children.

FRANCISCAN BENEDICTION

May God bless you with discomfort,
at easy answers, half-truths,
and superficial relationships
so that you may live
deep within your heart.
May God bless you with anger
at injustice, oppression,
and exploitation of people,
so that you may work for
justice, freedom and peace.
May God bless you with tears,
to shed for those who suffer pain,
rejection, hunger, and war,
so that you may reach out your hand
to comfort them and
to turn their pain to joy.
And may God bless you
with enough foolishness
to believe that you can
make a difference in the world,
so that you can do
what others claim cannot be done,
to bring justice and kindness
to all our children and the poor. Amen.

WEEK 13

DATE ____________ TIME____________ PLACE ______________________________

OPENING RITUAL

Remember, parents, this is up to you and your creativity! Is it a song that you sing or listen to together? A "ready-set-go" team chant? A minute of jumping jacks to get out the wiggles? Try out some ways to make your meetings "official" and create a mood of openness and engagement.

PRAYER

Take sixty seconds to pray together. You can pray in silence, or you can recite a traditional prayer such as the Our Father or Hail Mary.

MISSION REVIEW

Ask someone to recite, write, or sing your family's mission statement.

VISION REVIEW

Read your vision statement aloud.

GOAL REVIEW

- What goal(s) are you working toward? ______________________________

  ____

- Does it still sound reasonable? ______________________________

  ____

- What systems or habits did you put into place to help you make progress? _______

  ____

- How did it go this week? ______________________________

  ____

- What things got in the way of progress this week? What things helped? ______________________________

- Do you need prompts or reminders? If so, how and where? ______________________________

- What things do you want to celebrate about the process this week? ______________________________

- Do you need to change your habits? Do you need to change your goal? ______________________________

- How can you support one another better next week? ______________________________

DISCOVER YOUR FAITH

If you're not walking or cooking during your family gatherings (remember, in chapter 4, tip 3, we discussed these as options), then this section, which is meant to provide food for thought each week, might be the perfect time to literally have some food — to share a snack or dessert. Food makes it more fun, right?

So … right about now, do you feel like you don't even know what you don't know about being Catholic? Join the club! I was in Sunday school when I was very small. I attended Catholic grade school for eight years, and went to church every weekend. But it wasn't until I became a book editor at OSV in my late twenties that I realized how little I actually knew about things like the Doctors of the Church, novenas, the *Catechism*, the Vatican, encyclicals, and a whole bunch of other stuff.

Going forward, this "Discover Your Faith" section each week is going to introduce you to a Catholic initiative, concept, or organization. If it's appropriate for the kids in your family, you can read it aloud together. Or you can paraphrase for little ones, or create an activity around the concept.

Why does this matter? Because when you know about your faith, it becomes personal. It's not a set of rules or a dress that you wear on Sundays. It's who you are.

And who you are is one of God's children. Even the grown-ups! We're his marvelous creation, loved wholly and infinitely. When he created each one of us, uniquely gifted, he had a plan that, if we tune in, will lead us to bigger satisfaction and joy than we could ever hope to attain on our own.

So, we're going to listen. Pray. Practice. And learn. Just make sure that you all learn together as a team. As a grown-up, this is a chance to admit what you don't know. Encourage questions. Figure it out together. I'll have plenty of resources for you along the way.

I'm still learning too, by the way. I had to learn a whole bunch of things to write this book. Planet Fitness has their "Judgement Free Zone®" — why not apply the same sentiment to your team effort to achieve your vision?

ENCOURAGEMENT

Saint Paul, who wrote a big chunk of the New Testament, had this to say in one of his letters: "But [the Lord] said to me, 'My grace is sufficient for you, for my power is made perfect in weakness.' I will all the more gladly boast of my weaknesses, that the power of Christ may rest upon me" (2 Corinthians 12:9).

If Saint Paul, an actual saint, is able to talk openly about all the ways in which he's not perfect, then we shouldn't be ashamed either, right? This section each week will provide tips and inspiration from motivational experts, educators, and exceptional people to help you in your quest for improvement.

Here's one to start: "Effective work is about moving toward the desired destination, and not necessarily about ensuring that nothing gets spilled or knocked over in the process," writes Deep Patel, a Forbes contributor, in "Why Perfection Is the Enemy of Done."[11] "Mistakes will happen. Missteps will occur. It's momentum that matters, and ensuring that time is not wasted obsessing over the little things that won't end up moving the needle anyway."

PRAYER

If you need some reassurance at this point, start with Isaiah 43:1–3, which also inspired one of my favorite songs from Mass, "Be Not Afraid," by Robert J. Dufford, SJ. God makes it clear that this is personal, that he loves us, and that we are his.

> But now thus says the LORD,
> he who created you, O Jacob,
>   he who formed you, O Israel:
> "Fear not, for I have redeemed you;
>   I have called you by name, you are mine.
> When you pass through the waters I will be with you;
>   and through the rivers, they shall not overwhelm you;
> when you walk through fire you shall not be burned,
>   and the flame shall not consume you.
> For I am the LORD your God,
>   the Holy One of Israel, your Savior."

This trust, support, and love are what your family can offer you when you've cultivated a strong sense of belonging (team) and identity. It's what we can all rest in, knowing that we're a part of God's family.

Then you can wrap up with a prayer like this:

Holy Spirit, please help us focus on getting better, not being perfect. Help us know where we should try harder, and what's not worth worrying about. Thank you for guiding us in this process, and give us each a little extra patience with one another and ourselves. Amen!

TEAM SPIRIT

WAIT! Don't just drift away from your family gathering. Close it out with some excitement and joy! Ways you could part with enthusiasm include:

- High-fives all around
- A group hug
- A cheer: "We're good and God is great!" "All for him!" "Way to go, Team Smith, bringing the glory!"
- A favorite song, bells, a tambourine, or some other happy noise
- A transition to a different family activity, like a game night or movie night

NOTES FOR NEXT TIME

So, everybody, what worked during this first family soiree? What didn't? Make some notes for next week. And make sure you've already set a date and time for next week.

____

____

____

____

____

____

____

WEEK 14

DATE ____________ TIME____________ PLACE ______________________________

OPENING RITUAL

Remember, parents, this is up to you and your creativity! Is it a song that you sing or listen to together? A "ready-set-go" team chant? A minute of jumping jacks to get out the wiggles? Try out some ways to make your meetings "official" and create a mood of openness and engagement.

PRAYER

Take sixty seconds to pray together. You can pray in silence, or you can recite a traditional prayer such as the Our Father or Hail Mary.

MISSION REVIEW

Ask someone to recite, write, or sing your family's mission statement.

VISION REVIEW

Read your vision statement aloud.

GOAL REVIEW

- What goal(s) are you working toward? ________________________________

  ____

- Does it still sound reasonable?___________________________________

  ____

- What systems or habits did you put into place to help you make progress? _______

  ____

- How did it go this week? ____

  ____

- What things got in the way of progress this week? What things helped? ___________

____

- Do you need prompts or reminders? If so, how and where? ___________________

____

- What things do you want to celebrate about the process this week? ______________

____

- Do you need to change your habits? Do you need to change your goal? ___________

____

- How can you support one another better next week? _________________________

____

DISCOVER YOUR FAITH

I live near the mountains in Denver, Colorado. And every time I walk past my window with a view to the west, I pause and drink in the beauty of the Rockies.

Some people who grew up here don't notice the mountains very often anymore. Those majestic peaks become part of the scenery. But I grew up in Indiana, where things are very flat. To me, the natural wonder outside my window is glorious every day. I notice.

JUST AS YOU'RE A PART OF YOUR FAMILY RIGHT HERE, YOU'RE ALSO A PART OF GOD'S FAMILY. NO MATTER WHAT.

The fact that God sent his Son to become a man and die for our sins because he loved us so very much is sometimes like the view outside our window. It's always been there, something that everybody knows, and we don't even stop to think about it.

This is your invitation to stop. Look out the window — for real, if you want to. Notice.

When it sits with you for a minute, it becomes overwhelming, doesn't it? God loves you — each of you, and everyone whom he created — so very much that he has offered you a way to be close to him again, even when you mess up. Even when you sin. He sent Jesus to teach us about him, to be an example of how to live, and then to die for us. God opened the door.

And our faith is the way in.

We've talked a little bit about our faith so far, and how we're created to live the way that God planned for us. This year, you're going to learn about your faith, and you're going to live it with your mission, vision, and goals.

But first, pause and think about what kind of love God has for you. It's bigger than the love from anyone you know. Just as you're a part of your family right here, you're also a part of God's family. No matter what.

It's beautiful, isn't it? And it's the whole point. When you encounter something so grand, so incredible, you just have to respond. To tell someone. To go and see. To pause, look, listen, and fill up your heart. Faith is how we respond. God's infinite love is why.

ENCOURAGEMENT

In week 1, we talked about your family's "why." The first part of that "why" is: Why did God create you and your family in your unique and special way? Thinking about that helped you develop your mission.

The second part of your family's "why" is why you would try to figure out your mission at all. Why do any of it? That's where soaking up God's giant, beautiful, amazing love comes in. When you actually consider it and embrace it, you can't imagine doing anything else.

When you know these two "whys," you really can't go wrong. When you're listening to God and trying to live according to his plan, you'll find the peace that comes from him. It might not be easy — in fact, the apostles would be the first to tell you just how difficult following God can be. But he will be with you. As 1 John 5:2–4 says, "By this we know that we love the children of God, when we love God and obey his commandments. For this is the love of God, that we keep his commandments. And his commandments are not burdensome. For whatever is born of God overcomes the world."

PRAYER

Today, read this verse, then think about it for a minute. Sit with it for at least sixty seconds. Notice it:

> For God so loved the world that he gave his only-begotten Son, that whoever believes in him should not perish but have eternal life. For God sent the Son into the world, not to condemn the world, but that the world might be saved through him. (John 3:16–17)

TEAM SPIRIT

Close out your family meeting with some excitement and joy!

NOTES FOR NEXT TIME

WEEK 15

DATE ____________ TIME____________ PLACE ______________________________

OPENING RITUAL

Remember, parents, this is up to you and your creativity! Is it a song that you sing or listen to together? A "ready-set-go" team chant? A minute of jumping jacks to get out the wiggles? Try out some ways to make your meetings "official" and create a mood of openness and engagement.

PRAYER

Take sixty seconds to pray together. You can pray in silence, or you can recite a traditional prayer such as the Our Father or Hail Mary.

MISSION REVIEW

Ask someone to recite, write, or sing your family's mission statement.

VISION REVIEW

Read your vision statement aloud.

GOAL REVIEW

- What goal(s) are you working toward? ______________________________

  ____

- Does it still sound reasonable? ______________________________

  ____

- What systems or habits did you put into place to help you make progress? _______

  ____

- How did it go this week? ______________________________

  ____

- What things got in the way of progress this week? What things helped? ____________

  ____

- Do you need prompts or reminders? If so, how and where? ____________

  ____

- What things do you want to celebrate about the process this week? ____________

  ____

- Do you need to change your habits? Do you need to change your goal? ____________

  ____

- How can you support one another better next week? ____________

  ____

DISCOVER YOUR FAITH

You might not know that there is water underground in the desert until you see the palms.

An oasis is a place in the desert where fresh water, running underground, comes to the surface. There, it makes the ground able to grow plants, such as date palms, which are flowering palm trees that grow sweet dates. You may not see the water, but you can definitely enjoy the fruit.

God's grace is a little bit like that water under the sand. It comes freely, and it sparks life. Just as water helps the palm develop a root system to absorb even more water and grow stronger, God's grace makes us able to accept his forgiveness and grow as his children. And just as water eventually allows the palm to bear fruit, God's grace makes it possible for us to bear fruit — generosity, kindness, patience, and more. God's grace makes it possible for us to become the good people that he calls us to be.

There's a lot more about different kinds of grace in the *Catechism*, especially in chapter 3. (And there's a lot more about the amazing date palm and oases on the San Diego Zoo website and the National Geographic Resource Library site, respectively.)

What's really amazing though? God's grace is a river that never runs dry. Never. Whenever we go looking for more, we'll find it. There's nothing on this earth like it. There's no one on earth offering forgiveness like God.

ENCOURAGEMENT

If you're struggling to keep up with the goals that you've set and the habits that you've established, rest assured that you have some supernatural support. As Saint Augustine put it: "It is not that we keep His commandments first, and that then He loves; but that He loves us, and then we keep His commandments. This is that grace, which is revealed to the humble, but hidden from the proud."

God's love, his grace, gives us far more power to do the right thing than we'd have on our own. The Holy Spirit transforms us — first through the sacraments, but also through the everyday happenings in our lives — into people who want to do the right thing, and have more strength to do the right thing.

And then, in turn, by doing the right thing, we can merit the grace to spend eternity in heaven with God.

So, the next time you feel depleted or overwhelmed, say a quick prayer like the one below for an extra measure of grace.

PRAYER

Dear God, thanks for sending me enough grace to do the things that I need to do. I know that I don't do it alone. "But by the grace of God I am what I am, and his grace toward me was not in vain. On the contrary, I worked harder than any of them, though it was not I, but the grace of God which is with me" (1 Corinthians 15:10).

TEAM SPIRIT

Close out your family meeting with some excitement and joy!

NOTES FOR NEXT TIME

____

____

____

____

____

____

____

____

WEEK 16

DATE ____________ TIME____________ PLACE ______________________________

OPENING RITUAL

Remember, parents, this is up to you and your creativity! Is it a song that you sing or listen to together? A "ready-set-go" team chant? A minute of jumping jacks to get out the wiggles? Try out some ways to make your meetings "official" and create a mood of openness and engagement.

> ### PRAYER
> Take sixty seconds to pray together. You can pray in silence, or you can recite a traditional prayer such as the Our Father or Hail Mary.

MISSION REVIEW

Ask someone to recite, write, or sing your family's mission statement.

VISION REVIEW

Read your vision statement aloud.

GOAL REVIEW

- What goal(s) are you working toward? ______________________________

  ____

- Does it still sound reasonable? ______________________________________

  ____

- What systems or habits did you put into place to help you make progress? _______

  ____

- How did it go this week? ____

  ____

- What things got in the way of progress this week? What things helped?__________

  ____

- Do you need prompts or reminders? If so, how and where? ____________________

  ____

- What things do you want to celebrate about the process this week? _____________

  ____

- Do you need to change your habits? Do you need to change your goal? __________

  ____

- How can you support one another better next week? ________________________

  ____

DISCOVER YOUR FAITH

There are several key ways in which the Catholic Faith is different from other religions. At the heart of those is the way in which we meet Jesus.

Every time we receive the Eucharist, though it looks and tastes like bread and wine, we are receiving the actual Body and Blood of Jesus. At the consecration during Mass, when the priest says the words of Jesus over the bread and wine, they are truly changed into Jesus. The Church calls this change "transubstantiation."

This has been a part of our faith since the Last Supper, when Jesus took the bread and wine and said that we should take his Body and Blood, and do this in memory of him. As we know, shortly after this Jesus died on the cross, washing away our sins and opening up the door to heaven for his followers. What a gift!

THERE ARE SEVERAL KEY WAYS IN WHICH THE CATHOLIC FAITH IS DIFFERENT FROM OTHER RELIGIONS. AT THE HEART OF THOSE IS THE WAY IN WHICH WE MEET JESUS.

It's incredible to think that each of us today can take part in this experience. It wasn't limited to the apostles, long ago. We encounter the Real Presence of Jesus each time we receive the Eucharist. We can also spend time in his presence during Eucharistic adoration at our churches.

You probably experience Jesus in many ways as you go about your day. You might see signs of his grace in a kind stranger, or in a beautiful sunset. But the Eucharist is special and powerful.

It's your chance to sit with him at the table, along with all the other Catholics around the world.

Why? Because he loves us that much. Jesus didn't leave on the day he ascended into heaven. He is still with us right here on Earth, until we join him in heaven.

How does this fit in with your family's mission, vision, and goals? If you want to grow closer to Jesus, attending Eucharistic adoration is a way to feel surrounded by his love. If you want to bring other people closer to Jesus, you might bring the Eucharist to the sick, or become a minister of the Eucharist at church. Knowing what a gift you receive in the Eucharist, you might find yourself living more joyfully and sharing the Good News.

PRAYER

In his Gospel, John tells us how Jesus explained this to the apostles before the Last Supper. Read this passage together, and then use your own words to thank God for the chance to experience the Real Presence of Jesus and enter into heaven:

> So Jesus said to them, "Truly, truly, I say to you, unless you eat the flesh of the Son of man and drink his blood, you have no life in you; he who eats my flesh and drinks my blood has eternal life, and I will raise him up at the last day. For my flesh is food indeed, and my blood is drink indeed. He who eats my flesh and drinks my blood abides in me, and I in him. As the living Father sent me, and I live because of the Father, so he who eats me will live because of me." (John 6:53–57)

NOTES FOR NEXT TIME

____

____

____

____

____

____

____

WEEK 17

DATE ____________ TIME____________ PLACE ______________________________

OPENING RITUAL

Remember, parents, this is up to you and your creativity! Is it a song that you sing or listen to together? A "ready-set-go" team chant? A minute of jumping jacks to get out the wiggles? Try out some ways to make your meetings "official" and create a mood of openness and engagement.

PRAYER

Take sixty seconds to pray together. You can pray in silence, or you can recite a traditional prayer such as the Our Father or Hail Mary.

MISSION REVIEW

Ask someone to recite, write, or sing your family's mission statement.

VISION REVIEW

Read your vision statement aloud.

GOAL REVIEW

- What goal(s) are you working toward? ______________________________

  ____

- Does it still sound reasonable?___________________________________

  ____

- What systems or habits did you put into place to help you make progress? _______

  ____

- How did it go this week? ____

  ____

- What things got in the way of progress this week? What things helped? ____________

  ____

- Do you need prompts or reminders? If so, how and where? ____________________

  ____

- What things do you want to celebrate about the process this week? ______________

  ____

- Do you need to change your habits? Do you need to change your goal? ___________

  ____

- How can you support one another better next week? __________________________

  ____

DISCOVER YOUR FAITH

When we talked about God's amazing, incredible, never-ending grace in Week 15, I mentioned the *Catechism of the Catholic Church.*

Maybe you've heard of it through old-timey jokes about memorizing rules in Catholic school. And to glance at a copy of this thick book without a lot of pictures, you might be tempted to avoid it — or at least feel really intimidated by it.

But the *Catechism* is very useful as a one-stop shop for answers to everything Catholic. It takes all of the teachings of the Faith and puts them in one place. It helps explain parts of the Bible. It collects the best thinking of the smartest Catholic teachers and holiest saints over the centuries. You can look up the Catholic perspective on just about anything in the *Catechism.*

The current *Catechism of the Catholic Church* was updated in 1997. You can buy a print copy, or you can find it on the website of the United States Conference of Catholic Bishops. (See http://www.usccb.org/sites/default/files/flipbooks/catechism/.) Another easy way to look up things in the *Catechism* online is to search the text on the Vatican website at https://www.vatican.va/archive/ENG0015/_INDEX.HTM.

It's organized by paragraphs, so when you see a reference to something from the *Catechism,* it might look like "CCC 2205" (which, by the way, says in part, "The Christian family has an evangelizing and missionary task"). So 2205 is the paragraph number, not the page number. And if you know which paragraph number you're looking for, you can Google *Catechism + the paragraph number* to go right to that section in the Vatican website.

If your family's mission and vision include learning more about your faith, the *Catechism* is a good foundational resource. Granted, it's pretty thick reading. But it's helpful to at least understand what the *Catechism* is, because you'll see references to it in lots of other Catholic material.

There's also youcat.org, which has resources for families and kids, and *A Pocket Catechism for Kids* (Fr. Kris D. Stubna and Mike Aquilina) from OSV — parents, don't be shy about starting with this version yourselves!

ENCOURAGEMENT

Feeling like there's JUST SO MUCH? So much to do, so much to learn, so much to know?

Consider the idea of the "Minimum Viable Motivator," a concept floated by productivity writer Mark Sturm in "A Universal Formula for Doing Big Things."[12] With this strategy, you're only responsible for doing the smallest thing that (a) moves you toward a more difficult goal, while being both (b) easy and (c) pleasurable. Every time you do that smallest thing, you get better at it, and better equipped to do more. At the same time, making sure it's easy enough allows you to enjoy those little successes and motivates you to keep trying until, step by baby step, you've scaled the mountain.

What is one small, simple, easy thing you can do to move toward your goal in the next five minutes? Is it just making a sticky note so that you remember to do the next small, easy thing tomorrow? Try to do some minimal thing. It will make you feel as if you've made progress, and you'll feel motivated to continue.

PRAYER

Part four, section one of the *Catechism*, which talks about prayer, includes a great quote from St. Thérèse of Lisieux: "For me, prayer is a surge of the heart; it is a simple look turned toward heaven, it is a cry of recognition and of love, embracing both trial and joy" (2558).

> Dear God, when we feel overwhelmed, help us remember to turn toward heaven and offer whatever we're doing to you with love. And give us confidence that in that moment, that is enough. Amen!

TEAM SPIRIT

Close out your family meeting with some excitement and joy!

NOTES FOR NEXT TIME

WEEK 18

DATE ____________ TIME____________ PLACE ______________________________

OPENING RITUAL

Remember, parents, this is up to you and your creativity! Is it a song that you sing or listen to together? A "ready-set-go" team chant? A minute of jumping jacks to get out the wiggles? Try out some ways to make your meetings "official" and create a mood of openness and engagement.

PRAYER

Take sixty seconds to pray together. You can pray in silence, or you can recite a traditional prayer such as the Our Father or Hail Mary.

MISSION REVIEW

Ask someone to recite, write, or sing your family's mission statement.

VISION REVIEW

Read your vision statement aloud.

GOAL REVIEW

- What goal(s) are you working toward? ________________________________

  ____

- Does it still sound reasonable?____________________________________

  ____

- What systems or habits did you put into place to help you make progress? ______

  ____

- How did it go this week? ____

  ____

- What things got in the way of progress this week? What things helped? __________

____

- Do you need prompts or reminders? If so, how and where? ____________________

____

- What things do you want to celebrate about the process this week? ______________

____

- Do you need to change your habits? Do you need to change your goal? __________

____

- How can you support one another better next week? __________________________

____

DISCOVER YOUR FAITH

Quick, without looking: Do you know which version of the Bible you're using?

It's OK if you don't, but there are several Catholic versions — the *New American Bible, Revised Edition* (NABRE), for example, or the *Revised Standard Version, Catholic Edition* (RSVCE), which is used in this book.

If you ever want to check out the various versions and see how they differ, go to Bible Gateway (biblegateway.com) and type in a passage — say, for example, Matthew 6:26. If you've selected the RSVCE as your translation, you can scroll down and click on "Matthew 6:26 in all English translations" to see how the wording of that verse changes in other translations.

IMAGINING YOUR INCREDIBLE OUTCOME CAN REIGNITE THE SPARK OF ENTHUSIASM THAT YOU STARTED WITH.

And if you're curious about what's right before or right after this verse, click on "Read full chapter" under the verse.

You don't have to type a specific Bible verse into the search bar at Bible Gateway; you can also type in a simple word or phrase and see what passages are related to that topic anywhere in that translation. I love using this tool when I vaguely remember a phrase from the Bible, but not where it's from or the exact wording. It also leads me to other passages. See what you can discover with a bit of searching!

ENCOURAGEMENT

It's a good thing that I like going for long walks through lush landscapes, because I'm a terrible golfer. I end up traversing every inch of a course, including parts no one has ever seen or mowed.

So, when I prepare to hit a golf ball, I try to tick off every tip I've ever been taught — shoulders back, head down, eyes on the ball, knees bent, grip loose ... I'm so focused on my form that I forget to look for the flag. Sometimes I have to turn and face a different way and start all over.

Most of the time I just laugh at myself. But I'd do well also to keep in mind the words of author and motivational speaker Rachel Hollis: "There is so much power in focusing on the outcome you're after, instead of the to-do list you have in your mind," Hollis says in her *Rise* podcast.[13]

Not only can focusing on your vision help you ensure that you're headed in the right direction, even amid all the details and doing, but it can also be a great source of motivation. Imagining your incredible outcome can reignite the spark of enthusiasm that you started with. So, spend a moment envisioning the change you're working toward. Create a vision board, if a tangible reminder is even more powerful. You're still on your way!

PRAYER

One of my favorite Bible passages is Matthew 6:25–34. You can open your family Bible, or use the Bible Gateway tool to look it up. Read it together, then pray:

> God, you reassure us that you know all our needs and will provide for us. Thank you for your extraordinary love and unending care. Help us to rely on our faith, instead of being anxious. Amen!

TEAM SPIRIT

Close out your family meeting with some excitement and joy!

NOTES FOR NEXT TIME

WEEK 19

DATE ____________ TIME____________ PLACE ______________________

OPENING RITUAL

Remember, parents, this is up to you and your creativity! Is it a song that you sing or listen to together? A "ready-set-go" team chant? A minute of jumping jacks to get out the wiggles? Try out some ways to make your meetings "official" and create a mood of openness and engagement.

PRAYER

Take sixty seconds to pray together. You can pray in silence, or you can recite a traditional prayer such as the Our Father or Hail Mary.

MISSION REVIEW

Ask someone to recite, write, or sing your family's mission statement.

VISION REVIEW

Read your vision statement aloud.

DISCOVER YOUR FAITH

Are you reading this on a Sunday?

Sunday is a special day … and not just because our family would always get fresh doughnuts at Tom's Bakery after church when I was a little girl.

As the *Catechism* says, "Sunday, the 'Lord's Day,' is the principal day for the celebration of the Eucharist because it is the day of the Resurrection. It is the pre-eminent day of the liturgical assembly, the day of the Christian family, and the day of joy and rest from work. Sunday is 'the foundation and kernel of the whole liturgical year'" (1193).

I don't know about you, but the third commandment (Remember to keep holy the Lord's Day) felt like a huge guilt trip to me as a parent. For one thing, I didn't always have the luxury of not working on Sundays. Sometimes I was scheduled for a shift, and sometimes I had freelance work. If I weren't working for pay, I'd still have a billion chores to get done on the weekends — cleaning the house, mowing, grocery shopping, meal prep for the week, laundry, homework help … you know — because I had to work away from home every other day.

My kiddo usually had plenty to do as well. She was an essential part of keeping our household running, doing her own chores. And she had heaps of homework, which was a slog with her ADHD.

Let's just say we weren't lying in hammocks praying and resting on Sundays.

We did, however, make time for church, whether Saturday night or Sunday morning. And we had pancakes, which became a tradition for the two of us, much like doughnuts with my parents. The day was special, and God was a part of it.

Rest can also be an active thing. It can be a walk out in nature, wondering at God's creation. It can be restorative to listen to beautiful music, or to admire beautiful art. Joy for you could look like engaging in a hobby or sports. It might be a bit of silence in your household, or it might be interacting with others. The *Catechism* reminds us:

> Those Christians who have leisure should be mindful of their brethren who have the same needs and the same rights, yet cannot rest from work because of poverty and misery. Sunday is traditionally consecrated by Christian piety to good works and humble service of the sick, the infirm, and the elderly. Christians will also sanctify Sunday by devoting time and care to their families and relatives, often difficult to do on other days of the week. Sunday is a time for reflection, silence, cultivation of the mind, and meditation which furthers the growth of the Christian interior life. (2186)

Perhaps your family soirees are the way you make Sundays special in your house. Or maybe you get doughnuts after Mass. (Could you drop some off at my place while you're at it?) The point is not to make life harder by putting on hold the things about which you don't really have a choice. Instead, see how you can acknowledge God on this "day that the Lord has made" (1166). Bring him into everything you do.

ENCOURAGEMENT

Time management professional Laura Vanderkam has all kinds of grace for us in her *Medium* article "3 Times a Week Is a Habit."[14] When trying to cultivate a habit, she says we should forget aiming for "daily." Life gets in the way of daily, after all. And if you've held yourself to a standard of daily, you're doomed to fail. How many days will you fail before you throw in the towel altogether? (About six weeks, if you're the average New Year's Day gym-goer.)

Vanderkam suggests that we aim for three times in seven days. If you can hit that mark with regularity, you've got a bona fide habit on your hands. I'd say this even lets you scoot those seven days around if needed — move a weekend forward to next week or backward to last week, if it helps you achieve three times.

Shoot for consistency. Eating dinner together three times a week is way better than throwing in the dish towel.

PRAYER

Prayerfully read this Scripture passage — it's great for any day, but especially Sundays:

> This is the day which the Lord has made;
> let us rejoice and be glad in it. (Psalm 118:24).

TEAM SPIRIT

Close out your family meeting with some excitement and joy!

NOTES FOR NEXT TIME

WEEK 20

DATE ____________ TIME____________ PLACE ______________________________

OPENING RITUAL

Remember, parents, this is up to you and your creativity! Is it a song that you sing or listen to together? A "ready-set-go" team chant? A minute of jumping jacks to get out the wiggles? Try out some ways to make your meetings "official" and create a mood of openness and engagement.

> **PRAYER**
>
> Take sixty seconds to pray together. You can pray in silence, or you can recite a traditional prayer such as the Our Father or Hail Mary.

MISSION REVIEW

Ask someone to recite, write, or sing your family's mission statement.

VISION REVIEW

Read your vision statement aloud.

DISCOVER YOUR FAITH

When we're getting ready to eat, we make the Sign of the Cross reeeeeeallly fast. We just tack it on to the end of our mealtime blessing: FatherSonHolySpiritAmen.

But when you slow it down, there's a lot packed into a few words! I can't explain the symbolism behind it as well as Father Rocky does in "Catholic 101: The Sign of the Cross" on Relevant Radio's YouTube channel, so go check that out. The video is literally a minute. I'll wait …

What I can do is suggest ways to make the Sign of the Cross a part of your daily life.

When I was little and afraid of noises in the dark, I'd make the Sign of the Cross, creating what I imagined was a force field as strong as God between me and any evil spirits. When my daughter was little, I would bless her every night at bedtime with the Sign of the Cross, giving her a "force field," too.

You can pray the Sign of the Cross when you're feeling anxious or nervous, or when you need strength or comfort. You can speak the words, or you can simply make the gesture. It's a fantastic way to quickly reconnect with God.

WAS ONE OF YOUR GOALS OR HABITS THIS YEAR TO PRAY MORE OFTEN? THE SIGN OF THE CROSS COUNTS. IT'S A WAY TO TALK TO THE FATHER, THE SON, AND THE HOLY SPIRIT AT ANY TIME.

When I was growing up, we had a small, wall-mounted, guardian angel holy water font. Sometimes I'd dip in my fingers and make the Sign of the Cross as I went to my room down the hall, and it always felt extra special to have something from church right there in our house. If your family is seeking ways to connect more frequently with God, adding a holy water font is one simple way to bring him to mind and heart.

Was one of your goals or habits this year to pray more often? The Sign of the Cross counts. It's a way to talk to the Father, the Son, and the Holy Spirit at any time.

ENCOURAGEMENT

If you ever feel too old, too young, too busy, too small, too poor, too fill-in-the-blank to be able to achieve greatness, just think of Barbara Hillary.

Barbara Hillary was born in New York in 1931, and raised by her mother after her father died when she was a toddler. She had a long career in nursing and overcame cancer twice, surviving breast cancer in her twenties and lung cancer in her sixties. She lost twenty-five percent of her breathing capacity after surgery to treat the latter.

All of this was remarkable on its own, but it's what she did next that earned her even greater recognition.

After retirement, she became interested in travel to the Arctic. When she learned that no Black woman had reached the North Pole, she decided she'd be the first. At age seventy-five, she raised the money to fund an expedition, and in 2007 became the first Black woman and one of the oldest people to ever make the difficult journey.

Five years later, she tacked on several more firsts, making the trek to the South Pole at the age of seventy-nine. Barbara Hillary undertook an expedition across Mongolia as well before she passed away in 2019 at the age of eighty-eight. This amazing woman faced a lot of obstacles: age, race, health, finances. And yet she was inspirational! You can read all about her at barbarahillary.com.

If you feel like there's a "too" standing in your way, remember Barbara Hillary. Perhaps God is presenting you with challenges so that you too can be an inspiration to others.

PRAYER

Take some time to slowly pray the Sign of the Cross. Simply say the words, and pause after each line, taking fifteen to thirty seconds to absorb the meaning and to connect deeply with the Father, the Son, and the Holy Spirit. Amen!

TEAM SPIRIT

Close out your family meeting with some excitement and joy!

NOTES FOR NEXT TIME

WEEK 21

DATE ____________ TIME______________ PLACE __________________________________

OPENING RITUAL

Remember, parents, this is up to you and your creativity! Is it a song that you sing or listen to together? A "ready-set-go" team chant? A minute of jumping jacks to get out the wiggles? Try out some ways to make your meetings "official" and create a mood of openness and engagement.

PRAYER

Take sixty seconds to pray together. You can pray in silence, or you can recite a traditional prayer such as the Our Father or Hail Mary.

MISSION REVIEW

Ask someone to recite, write, or sing your family's mission statement.

VISION REVIEW

Read your vision statement aloud.

GOAL REVIEW

- What goal(s) are you working toward? ____________________________________

  ____

- Does it still sound reasonable? ____

  ____

- What systems or habits did you put into place to help you make progress? _______

  ____

- How did it go this week? ____

  ____

- What things got in the way of progress this week? What things helped?___________

____

- Do you need prompts or reminders? If so, how and where? ____________________

____

- What things do you want to celebrate about the process this week? ______________

____

- Do you need to change your habits? Do you need to change your goal? ___________

____

- How can you support one another better next week? __________________________

____

DISCOVER YOUR FAITH

There are so many ways to pray. As a Catholic, you probably know some formal prayers, right? Of course, there's the classic Our Father, which comes straight from Jesus, who told his followers:

> Your Father knows what you need before you ask him. Pray then like this:
> Our Father who art in heaven,
> Hallowed be thy name.
> Thy kingdom come,
> Thy will be done,
> On earth as it is in heaven.
> Give us this day our daily bread;
> And forgive us our trespasses,
> As we forgive those who trespass against us;
> And lead us not into temptation,
> But deliver us from evil. (Matthew 6:8–13)

You can lean on the Our Father whenever you need to offer up a prayer. But did you also realize that you can just talk to God the Father, or Jesus, or the Holy Spirit? And that you should listen, too?

I talk differently with each Person of the Trinity — God the Father, Jesus the Son, and the Holy Spirit. Each is equally important. But I find that my conversation changes.

To me, God the Father is the mighty figure I hear in the Old Testament. When I think of the Father, I think of awe and thunder, worship and praise and glory. I approach him with respect, and even a bit of fear. When I'm hiking in the mountains, and my heart is ready to explode with wonder, I thank God the Father.

To me, Jesus the Son is the man I hear in the New Testament. He's always provocative, and always relevant. I look to him for inspiration in my daily life. Especially in difficult situations, I ask him, "How would you handle this? What would you say about this situation?"

To me, the Holy Spirit is the voice I hear within. He is whispers and thoughts. The warmth of love. The crackle of energy. The Holy Spirit is wind, moving me in the right direction. For me, the Holy Spirit is very personal.

So, that's how I pray. How do you pray? There is no wrong way — only more right ways to add to what you already do. Worship. Praise. Plead. Read. Learn. Listen. Ask. Thank. Wonder. Sit with the breath of the Holy Spirit rushing through your lungs, inhaling and exhaling reassurance, love, fire, guidance, and peace.

In whatever ways you can, further your relationship with God the Father, Jesus the Son, and the Holy Spirit. Pray. Sing. Dance. Hike. Clean. Cook. Drive. Communicate with him in acts of service, or in utter silence.

ENCOURAGEMENT

Throughout this process of mission, vision, and goal setting, we've talked about setting up habits to help you make progress. But maybe it's more helpful for you to think of them as practices.

"Although daily routines are important and many of us rely on them, the truth is that routines are fragile," Ryan Holiday writes. "Practices are different. Practices are things you do regularly — perhaps daily, perhaps not — but in no particular order. They are things you return to, time and time again, to center yourself. To reset. To reconnect. To focus. … One is about daily rhythm, while the other is a lifelong pursuit."[15]

Prayer can be like this. It can be a routine, sure. Maybe you have a morning routine that includes prayer, or a prayer routine at mealtime, at bedtime, or during goodbyes. Awesome! But prayer might also be a practice. It might be something you turn to when you don't know where else to turn. If you find yourself out of sorts, confused, worried, blissfully happy, or feeling in some other way full of emotion or thoughts, try taking a minute to pray.

This makes prayer a tool, instead of a to-do. Rather than adding to your checklist, prayer can add to your peace.

(By the way, if kiddos need a guide to prayer and talking to God, I wrote the *Catholic Prayer Book for Children* a few years ago. You can order it at OSV.com.)

PRAYER

Make up your own this week. Talk to God the Father, Jesus the Son, and the Holy Spirit!

TEAM SPIRIT

Close out your family meeting with some excitement and joy!

NOTES FOR NEXT TIME

WEEK 22

DATE ____________ TIME____________ PLACE ______________________________

OPENING RITUAL

Remember, parents, this is up to you and your creativity! Is it a song that you sing or listen to together? A "ready-set-go" team chant? A minute of jumping jacks to get out the wiggles? Try out some ways to make your meetings "official" and create a mood of openness and engagement.

PRAYER

Take sixty seconds to pray together. You can pray in silence, or you can recite a traditional prayer such as the Our Father or Hail Mary.

MISSION REVIEW

Ask someone to recite, write, or sing your family's mission statement.

VISION REVIEW

Read your vision statement aloud.

GOAL REVIEW

- What goal(s) are you working toward? ______________________________

  ____

- Does it still sound reasonable?______________________________

  ____

- What systems or habits did you put into place to help you make progress? _______

  ____

- How did it go this week? ______________________________

  ____

- What things got in the way of progress this week? What things helped? ___________

  ____

- Do you need prompts or reminders? If so, how and where? ____________________

  ____

- What things do you want to celebrate about the process this week? ______________

  ____

- Do you need to change your habits? Do you need to change your goal? ___________

  ____

- How can you support one another better next week? _________________________

  ____

DISCOVER YOUR FAITH

When I was growing up, one of the most confusing things for my non-Catholic friends to understand was why we prayed to Mary. They thought that we worshiped her, like we worship Jesus (not true). But she does hold a special place in our hearts.

There's a lot to know about Mary, so we won't talk about it all right now. But here are some highlights:

- The Immaculate Conception does not refer to Mary and Jesus. Rather, it's the teaching that Mary was born without original sin — the sin that we've all been born with since Adam and Eve ate the apple. We celebrate Mary's Immaculate Conception on December 8.
- We honor Mary as the Mother of God. With her "yes" to this monumental role, at great personal risk, she became an essential part of the story of Jesus as our Savior. We celebrate the feast of Mary Mother of God on January 1.
- We pray to Mary, asking her to intercede for us, just as we pray to the other saints. We ask her to join her prayers with ours to God.
- We especially look to her for help and guidance as a mother to us all.

One of my fondest memories as a little girl was taking flowers to school to place at the foot of the statue of Mary in church before Mother's Day. My own mother would help me clip some gloriously fragrant lilacs, wrap them in a damp paper towel, and then wrap that wet towel in foil. I'd carry the purple blossoms ever so carefully on the school bus, trying to protect them from jostles and the noses of curious public-school kids, soaking up the heady scent all the way. It felt so special bringing something of such great beauty to Mary, and to feel surrounded by her love. And I can't smell lilacs today without recalling that little-girl joy.

Introduce little ones to Mary with *The Story of Mary* coloring book; *Just Like Mary* (Rosemarie Gortler/Donna Piscitelli); or *Teach Me About Mary* (Joan Plum/Paul Plum/Catherine Odell), all from OSV.

ENCOURAGEMENT

If anyone was asked to do the impossible, it was Mary. She was still a human being, and yet she was told that her life was going to be turned upside down, that she was going to be pregnant without having a husband first, and that her baby was going to be the Son of God. All this from an angel, no less.

And yet, she said, "Let it be" (Luke 1:38).

TAKE A DEEP BREATH, ACKNOWLEDGE THAT SOMETIMES THINGS ARE DIFFICULT, LISTEN TO WHAT GOD IS ASKING OF YOU, AND SAY, "LET IT BE."

So, when you struggle with the things you're doing — or not doing — in order to improve your relationship with your family, your faith, your community, and God, remember Mary. Take a deep breath, acknowledge that sometimes things are difficult, listen to what God is asking of you, and say, "Let it be." There are buckets of fortitude, resiliency, and courage in those three small words.

PRAYER

The Hail Mary is the best-known Marian prayer, and the first half of the prayer comes right from Luke 1:26–45:

Hail Mary, full of grace,
the Lord is with you.
Blessed are you among women,
and blessed is the fruit of your womb, Jesus.
Holy Mary, Mother of God,
pray for us sinners,
now and at the hour of our death.
Amen.

TEAM SPIRIT

Close out your family meeting with some excitement and joy!

NOTES FOR NEXT TIME

WEEK 23

DATE ____________ TIME_____________ PLACE ______________________________

OPENING RITUAL

Remember, parents, this is up to you and your creativity! Is it a song that you sing or listen to together? A "ready-set-go" team chant? A minute of jumping jacks to get out the wiggles? Try out some ways to make your meetings "official" and create a mood of openness and engagement.

PRAYER

Take sixty seconds to pray together. You can pray in silence, or you can recite a traditional prayer such as the Our Father or Hail Mary.

MISSION REVIEW

Ask someone to recite, write, or sing your family's mission statement.

VISION REVIEW

Read your vision statement aloud.

GOAL REVIEW

- What goal(s) are you working toward? ______________________________

  ____

- Does it still sound reasonable? ____________________________________

  ____

- What systems or habits did you put into place to help you make progress? ______

  ____

- How did it go this week? ____

  ____

- What things got in the way of progress this week? What things helped?__________

____

- Do you need prompts or reminders? If so, how and where? __________________

____

- What things do you want to celebrate about the process this week? _____________

____

- Do you need to change your habits? Do you need to change your goal? _________

____

- How can you support one another better next week? _______________________

____

DISCOVER YOUR FAITH

When I was a little girl, if we arrived at church well before Mass, there were sometimes a handful of elderly women rattling off the prayers of the Rosary. It seemed to me like something that old people did, a series of prayers that I just had to memorize for school. And aside from admiring the sparkles of the beautiful beads with the engraved crucifix that my parents gave me for my First Communion, I didn't think much about it.

Then I started traveling to Europe, and I found rosaries to be gorgeous souvenirs of the majestic cathedrals all over the continent. I even bought a rosary bracelet with scrolled wooden beads from St. Mark's Basilica in Venice, and wore it often as a reminder of my first overseas adventure.

I happened to be wearing that one-decade rosary bracelet when I learned that someone in my family was in imminent danger. I was on an airplane that was closing its doors, so there was nothing I could do at the moment but pray. My mind was racing, but my fingers traveled along the beads, and it brought a sense of calm and peace to be able to meditate and focus.

I could explain how to pray the Rosary and the significance of each of the prayers, but Catholic Answers does a much better job. Take a look at www.catholic.com/tract/the-rosary. I also included a simple how-to for kids in my *Catholic Prayer Book for Children*.

The meditative quality of the Rosary, particularly when you contemplate the mysteries, is valuable when your heart and mind are having a hard time knowing what to say. And you definitely do not need to be elderly to appreciate it.

ENCOURAGEMENT

It's very tricky to start something new all by yourself. There's a reason why people who are quitting alcohol join AA, and there's a reason why people who are changing their eating habits join WW. "The key — if you want to build habits that last — is to join a group where the desired behavior is the normal behavior," writes James Clear in *Atomic Habits.*[16]

Similar to the adage that "you are who you surround yourself with," this is a reminder that you need more than willpower — you need a supportive team. The places you go, the ways you spend your time— all are influenced by your circle.

So, as you work toward your goals, find your people. Maybe your family — your team — is enough for each of you. Or maybe your family needs to find other families who have the same sort of interests and goals. It might be parishioners, fellow volunteers, or other clusters of people who share your passions and values. It's hard to swim upstream; find a group that's already making waves and hop in their canoe.

PRAYER

Pray the Rosary this week. If you don't have one in your house, you might spend this prayer time making one instead. You can easily find tutorials for praying the Rosary and for making a rosary online.

TEAM SPIRIT

Close out your family meeting with some excitement and joy!

NOTES FOR NEXT TIME

____

____

____

____

____

____

WEEK 24

DATE ____________ TIME____________ PLACE ______________________________

OPENING RITUAL

Remember, parents, this is up to you and your creativity! Is it a song that you sing or listen to together? A "ready-set-go" team chant? A minute of jumping jacks to get out the wiggles? Try out some ways to make your meetings "official" and create a mood of openness and engagement.

PRAYER

Take sixty seconds to pray together. You can pray in silence, or you can recite a traditional prayer such as the Our Father or Hail Mary.

MISSION REVIEW

Ask someone to recite, write, or sing your family's mission statement.

VISION REVIEW

Read your vision statement aloud.

GOAL REVIEW

- What goal(s) are you working toward? ______________________________

  ____

- Does it still sound reasonable? ______________________________

  ____

- What systems or habits did you put into place to help you make progress? _______

  ____

- How did it go this week? ______________________________

  ____

- What things got in the way of progress this week? What things helped?__________

  ____

- Do you need prompts or reminders? If so, how and where? __________________

  ____

- What things do you want to celebrate about the process this week? _____________

  ____

- Do you need to change your habits? Do you need to change your goal? __________

  ____

- How can you support one another better next week? ______________________

  ____

DISCOVER YOUR FAITH

When I was little, I was pretty surprised to learn that not everybody prayed to the saints; in fact, some religions don't even have saints. And some of my friends thought it was really weird to talk about saints. They thought that we worshiped them like we worship God.

I was much older when I learned how to address this with non-Catholics. I had to explain that when we pray to the saints, we're actually asking them to intercede — to talk to God on our behalf. It's a little bit like asking your friends to pray for you when you're facing something hopeful or uncertain.

Pope Francis writes:

> The great men and women of God were great intercessors. Intercession is like a "leaven" in the heart of the Trinity. It is a way of penetrating the Father's heart and discovering new dimensions which can shed light on concrete situations and change them. *We can say that God's heart is touched by our intercession, yet in reality he is always there first.* What our intercession achieves is that his power, his love and his faithfulness are shown ever more clearly in the midst of the people.[17]

Aside from their prayers on our behalf, another awesome thing about the saints is the fact that they were ordinary people, just like us, who did extraordinary things. So they're proof that, with God, we can achieve greatness. They didn't have superpowers or anything. They just made choices and lived

THE SAINTS MADE CHOICES AND LIVED LIVES THAT SHOWED INCREDIBLE COMMITMENT TO AND LOVE FOR GOD AND DOING HIS WILL. WE CAN, TOO!

lives that showed incredible commitment to and love for God and doing his will. We can, too!

Certain saints are known for certain things. When we lost things as kids, my mom and grandma always told us to pray to Saint Anthony. A member of the religious order called the Franciscans, a preacher, and a teacher, Saint Anthony of Padua was famous in the early 1200s for being a patron of the poor. He was eventually named a Doctor of the Church, meaning that he was recognized for his teaching and writing on theology and doctrine. Many people have experienced miracles after praying to Saint Anthony, which is how he also became famous for finding lost things. The next time you lose a book or your keys, ask him for a hand!

Consider finding saints to be your patrons — people to whom you can relate, or people who inspire you. You can find a wealth of information online, and there are plenty of books on the saints as well.

ENCOURAGEMENT

Am I the only one who finds it really hard to admit that I need help with something? I don't like to be a bother. I also enjoy figuring out things on my own — I feel resourceful. I love to learn new skills. And I feel like I owe it to everyone around me to at least attempt a task before I ask someone else for their time.

"Most people who have grown up in individualistic cultures like the United States are often raised with the belief that relying on others and asking for help is a burden to others and makes you seem emotionally weak," writes Dr. Joan Rosenberg. "Despite these views, there is ultimately very little that any of us do to succeed fully on our own, even if that is hard to acknowledge. You need both independence and dependence — not one or the other."[18]

So, if you're struggling with something — as an individual or a family — consider revealing your dependence and ask for a hand. Whether it's another family member, a friend or expert, or even a saint, tell someone where you're stuck. Sometimes even the act of explaining the issue leads you to new solutions. We're all part of one body, remember, with different roles and abilities. Don't be afraid to ask a foot for help with what you, as a hand, can't do!

PRAYER

Here's a formal prayer to Saint Anthony; you can also just ask him for his help in your own words whenever you need him:

> Saint Anthony, perfect imitator of Jesus, who received from God the special power of restoring lost things, grant that I may find (mention your petition), which has been

> lost. At least restore to me peace and tranquility of mind, the loss of which has afflicted me even more than my material loss.
>
> To this favor I ask another of you: that I may always remain in possession of the true good that is God. Let me rather lose all things than lose God, my supreme good. Let me never suffer the loss of my greatest treasure, eternal life with God. Amen.

TEAM SPIRIT

Close out your family meeting with some excitement and joy!

NOTES FOR NEXT TIME

____

____

____

____

____

____

____

____

WEEK 25

DATE ____________ TIME____________ PLACE ______________________________

OPENING RITUAL

Remember, parents, this is up to you and your creativity! Is it a song that you sing or listen to together? A "ready-set-go" team chant? A minute of jumping jacks to get out the wiggles? Try out some ways to make your meetings "official" and create a mood of openness and engagement.

PRAYER

Take sixty seconds to pray together. You can pray in silence, or you can recite a traditional prayer such as the Our Father or Hail Mary.

MISSION REVIEW

Ask someone to recite, write, or sing your family's mission statement.

VISION REVIEW

Read your vision statement aloud.

GOAL REVIEW

- What goal(s) are you working toward? ______________________________

  ____

- Does it still sound reasonable? ______________________________

  ____

- What systems or habits did you put into place to help you make progress? ________

  ____

- How did it go this week? ______________________________

  ____

- What things got in the way of progress this week? What things helped?__________

  ____

- Do you need prompts or reminders? If so, how and where? ____________________

  ____

- What things do you want to celebrate about the process this week? _____________

  ____

- Do you need to change your habits? Do you need to change your goal? __________

  ____

- How can you support one another better next week? _______________________

  ____

DISCOVER YOUR FAITH

The phrase "feast day" makes me imagine a plump, jolly king, sitting at his giant table, waving around a fat turkey leg, surrounded by platters heaping full of grapes, meat, potatoes, and cheese. Or it makes me think of doughnuts. My feast would be platters of doughnuts.

But the Catholic Church has a calendar full of feast days that don't have anything to do with food. Rather, they are times to celebrate the canonized saints — those ordinary people whose lives were so extraordinary that they've met all the criteria for sainthood in the Church.

Usually a saint's feast day is on the day he or she was born or died. Sometimes a feast day might mark something exceptional that happened in his or her life. Some are more well-known. (Ever hear of Saint Patrick's Day or Saint Valentine's Day?) Some are much more obscure. But each is recognized with a date on the calendar and possibly a prayer or Scripture reading. In fact, every day is the feast of a saint!

The Church has a lot more than 365 canonized saints, so many saints share a day. Do a bit of Googling right now to see whose feast day it is today. For a global perspective, visit https://www.catholicapostolatecenterfeastdays.org/. You can search to see which saints share your names or your birthdays. You might decide to add a celebration to your own calendar!

ENCOURAGEMENT

Writer, speaker, and entrepreneur James Clear writes, "It's better to do less than you hoped than nothing at all. No zero days."[19]

So maybe you had a bad day, or a busy day, and you failed to achieve your goal to pray before breakfast, perform an act of kindness for a stranger, or keep your cool when your kids were whiny. You can still save the day. What tiny thing can you do with the time that's left? Can you whisper a quick prayer before bed? Can you send an encouraging email to someone you haven't seen in a while? Can you apologize to your kids and ask for their forgiveness?

Forget perfection. Don't throw in the towel because you forgot. Do what you can. Tomorrow is a new day.

PRAYER

Dear God, you've sent the Holy Spirit to help so many of us ordinary people do extraordinary things. With you, all things are possible. God, you are mighty and magnificent!

TEAM SPIRIT

Close out your family meeting with some excitement and joy!

NOTES FOR NEXT TIME

____

____

____

____

____

____

____

____

WEEK 26

DATE ____________ TIME____________ PLACE ______________________________

OPENING RITUAL

Remember, parents, this is up to you and your creativity! Is it a song that you sing or listen to together? A "ready-set-go" team chant? A minute of jumping jacks to get out the wiggles? Try out some ways to make your meetings "official" and create a mood of openness and engagement.

PRAYER

Take sixty seconds to pray together. You can pray in silence, or you can recite a traditional prayer such as the Our Father or Hail Mary.

MISSION REVIEW

Ask someone to recite, write, or sing your family's mission statement.

VISION REVIEW

Read your vision statement aloud.

GOAL REVIEW

- What goal(s) are you working toward? ______________________________

  ____

- Does it still sound reasonable? ______________________________

  ____

- What systems or habits did you put into place to help you make progress? _______

  ____

- How did it go this week? ______________________________

  ____

- What things got in the way of progress this week? What things helped? ____________

____

- Do you need prompts or reminders? If so, how and where? ____________

____

- What things do you want to celebrate about the process this week? ____________

____

- Do you need to change your habits? Do you need to change your goal? ____________

____

- How can you support one another better next week? ____________

____

DISCOVER YOUR FAITH

Hey! Guess what?

We're at the halfway mark in your year-long adventure to become closer to God and one another. Think about how much you've learned, changed, and done since you started! This calls for a celebration. Look back at your kickoff party for inspiration. How can you incorporate some of the best elements?

Instead of the usual questions next week, come prepared to talk about the highlights of the journey. Identify some good traits or efforts that you observed in another member of your family. Think about the ways that your home, no matter who's in it or how you've all come to be together, has actually become that domestic church that we talked about before: "Thus the home is the first school of Christian life and 'a school for human enrichment.' Here one learns endurance and the joy of work, fraternal love, generous — even repeated — forgiveness, and above all divine worship in prayer and the offering of one's life" (CCC 1657).

Think too about the ways you've seen God's grace in your lives since you started. Are there times when you've experienced something that reminded you just how much God loves you? How much he loves those around you? Come prepared to talk about it.

Assess the goals that you set at the beginning of this process. Do they still fit you well? Do they need to be bigger, smaller, or more specific? This is a great time to refocus or shift gears for the remainder of your journey.

Next week may call for awards. Perhaps you'll want to watch a family movie or make a special meal. What about music? Decorations? Do it up! Make it happy and make it happen with the God-given brand of joy that moves your family!

ENCOURAGEMENT

"When we think of an achievement, we tend to picture something out of the ordinary, like exceeding targets, landing a big sale, or delivering a project milestone," the Mind Tools Content Team writes at MindTools.com. "But other, less measurable, behaviors deserve recognition, too — for example, pulling together as a team to head off a crisis, learning and applying a new skill, or supporting new recruits. Even something as simple as quietly consistent good work can be worthy of celebration."[20]

YOU DON'T HAVE TO HIT ALL THE MARKS TO CELEBRATE A WIN.

You don't have to hit all the marks to celebrate a win. Measure success with Carol Dweck's growth mindset. As she says: "It's critical to reward not just effort but learning and progress, and to emphasize the processes that yield these things, such as seeking help from others, trying new strategies, and capitalizing on setbacks to move forward effectively."

Does this help you rethink your successes? What are some examples of a growth mindset?

PRAYER

Read together Luke 8:4–8 below (the Parable of the Sower). This is a story from Jesus about how each of us responds to hearing the teachings of the Lord:

> And when a great crowd came together and people from town after town came to him, he said in a parable: "A sower went out to sow his seed; and as he sowed, some fell along the path, and was trodden under foot, and the birds of the air devoured it. And some fell on the rock; and as it grew up, it withered away, because it had no moisture. And some fell among thorns; and the thorns grew with it and choked it. And some fell into good soil and grew, and yielded a hundredfold." As he said this, he called out, "He who has ears to hear, let him hear."
>
> Dear God, we're working hard to listen to your call this year. Thank you for your grace, which helps to make our own hearts good soil where your love and your teaching can grow roots and be strong!

TEAM SPIRIT

Close out your family meeting with some excitement and joy!

NOTES FOR NEXT TIME

WEEK 27

DATE ____________ TIME____________ PLACE ______________________________

OPENING RITUAL

Remember, parents, this is up to you and your creativity! Is it a song that you sing or listen to together? A "ready-set-go" team chant? A minute of jumping jacks to get out the wiggles? Try out some ways to make your meetings "official" and create a mood of openness and engagement.

CELEBRATION

This week is special!

We're halfway through the year! Can you believe it? Give one another high-fives all around. Woohoo!

As you blaze into the second half of the year, take some time to make notes about the first half.

- Are you different from when you started this process? If so, how?
- Is your family different from when you started this process? If so, how?
- What are some of the most surprising things you've learned? The most interesting things you've done?
- What do you wish you knew before beginning this process? What do you wish you could do differently?
- How can you be a source of encouragement and support for your team?
- Where have you seen God's grace at work in your lives, or in the lives of others so far?

Need a pick-me-up? See if you can create a "how it started; how it's going" meme for your family adventure.

Take a minute, using words, drawings, or photos (image-editing platform Kapwing even has a template at www.kapwing.com/explore/how-it-started-vs-how-its-going-meme-template) to describe how your family relationship with one another and with God looked before you began your mission-vision-goals journey so long ago. Then compare it with how it's going. See a difference?

Take a break from your routine and find a way to celebrate. Record your family's activities, thoughts, and memories here.

____

____

____

ENCOURAGEMENT

Sometimes the best way to do something huge is to do nothing at all.

I realize that this sounds more like a persuasive tactic from a reluctant student than a motivational tip. But if you've ever listened to an elite athlete talking about his or her training, you'll realize that rest days are equally as important as work days. They're essential to avoiding burnout or injury. And in fact, rest days are when one's muscles knit themselves back together after the micro injuries of hard work, growing bigger and stronger. It's impossible to improve without rest.

Has your team been taking any rest days? Have you reached the point where working toward your goals feels like a slog? Are you allowing time to heal and grow stronger?

Maybe you need a rest day. Or a rest week. Talk amongst yourselves and see how everyone's feeling at this point in your journey. Then consider building in some days off so that you can hit the ground running (or jogging very slowly, if you're me) when you get back to it. This week, make time simply to appreciate being a part of your family, as well as God's.

PRAYER

Create your own prayer this week. What do you need from the Father, the Son, and the Holy Spirit as you look ahead to the second half of the year? Ask for it now. And offer praise and thanksgiving for the opportunity to have come this far. Amen.

TEAM SPIRIT

Close out your family meeting with some excitement and joy!

NOTES FOR NEXT TIME

WEEK 28

DATE ____________ TIME______________ PLACE ________________________________

OPENING RITUAL

Remember, parents, this is up to you and your creativity! Is it a song that you sing or listen to together? A "ready-set-go" team chant? A minute of jumping jacks to get out the wiggles? Try out some ways to make your meetings "official" and create a mood of openness and engagement.

PRAYER

Take sixty seconds to pray together. You can pray in silence, or you can recite a traditional prayer such as the Our Father or Hail Mary.

MISSION REVIEW

Ask someone to recite, write, or sing your family's mission statement.

VISION REVIEW

Read your vision statement aloud.

GOAL REVIEW

- What goal(s) are you working toward? ________________________________

  ____

- Does it still sound reasonable? ____________________________________

  ____

- What systems or habits did you put into place to help you make progress? _______

  ____

- How did it go this week? ____

  ____

- What things got in the way of progress this week? What things helped?__________

  ____

- Do you need prompts or reminders? If so, how and where? __________________

  ____

- What things do you want to celebrate about the process this week? _____________

  ____

- Do you need to change your habits? Do you need to change your goal? __________

  ____

- How can you support one another better next week? ______________________

  ____

DISCOVER YOUR FAITH

One of my favorite traditions is homemade strawberry pie on my birthday. Traditionally, my mom made it with sun-sweetened strawberries, fresh from our massive garden; more recently, my daughter took a turn (with dough from scratch!). I'm not a tradition-bound person, but there are certain traditions that stick. Pie is one of them.

When we talk about tradition in the Catholic Church, however, we're referring to the capital "T" Tradition. It's the peanut butter to the jelly of Scripture — both absolutely necessary.

While the Bible was written long after the events within had occurred, and has been subject to many translations over the centuries, Catholic Tradition is the understanding of the Faith as given to the very first apostles by Christ, and handed down orally to each generation thereafter.

In fact, the Gospel of John says, "Now Jesus did many other signs in the presence of the disciples, which are not written in this book; but these are written that you may believe that Jesus is the Christ, the Son of God, and that believing you may have life in his name" (20:30–31).

You can think of it like this: Catholic bishops can claim apostolic succession — each can trace his predecessor all the way back to the first apostles. Those apostles started teaching well before the New Testament was written down, and they and their successors eventually decided which sacred books belonged in the Bible. Jesus instructed and commissioned his apostles to personally teach the Faith … and that is Tradition.

It's like ham and eggs. Spaghetti and meatballs. Fish and chips. Each part is necessary to the whole that is our faith, and each elevates the other. The Church relies on Scripture and Tradition as the sources of our faith, and we need both.

IDENTIFYING WHAT MAKES YOUR FAITH UNIQUE IS ESSENTIAL TO LIVING IT AND PASSING IT ALONG.

This might help you understand where certain "Catholic things" come from, as you're strengthening your family team — your domestic church. You might come to realize that some of your values — the things that helped you create your mission and vision — are based upon Catholic Tradition. And identifying what makes your faith unique is essential to living it and passing it along.

I may feel as if my birthday strawberry pie is a tradition worthy of a capital T, but the Church's Tradition is truly an historic, vital, and sacred part of our Catholic Faith — a "birthday" gift handed down directly from Christ.

ENCOURAGEMENT

In my line of business, internal marketing is often an afterthought.

Sure, our team can create a killer new ad campaign for a company, carefully considering the creative, the audience, the platform, and execution. But the best ad in the world will fall flat if we fail to tell the company's staff about it. Because everyone, from the salesperson on the showroom floor to the customer service rep at the repair window, needs to be able to speak to the promises made in the advertising and represent the brand consistently.

Don't let this happen with your team — your family. If enthusiasm is flagging, think about how to reconnect your goals with your vision — the payoff. Give your family a pep talk and reinforce your mission. Do something fun that brings your mission to life: movies, games, music, food, play. All of this goes for adults and kids; anyone can be a brand ambassador.

Remember to nurture your internal marketing once in a while. As the old business axiom goes, your people are your greatest asset!

PRAYER

Holy Spirit, fill us with wisdom. We place our trust in the Tradition of the Church, as well as your word in Scripture. Thank you, God, for giving us these sources of your revelation, and for revealing your grace and calling to us!

TEAM SPIRIT

Close out your family meeting with some excitement and joy!

NOTES FOR NEXT TIME

WEEK 29

DATE ____________ TIME____________ PLACE ________________________________

OPENING RITUAL

Remember, parents, this is up to you and your creativity! Is it a song that you sing or listen to together? A "ready-set-go" team chant? A minute of jumping jacks to get out the wiggles? Try out some ways to make your meetings "official" and create a mood of openness and engagement.

PRAYER

Take sixty seconds to pray together. You can pray in silence, or you can recite a traditional prayer such as the Our Father or Hail Mary.

MISSION REVIEW

Ask someone to recite, write, or sing your family's mission statement.

VISION REVIEW

Read your vision statement aloud.

GOAL REVIEW

- What goal(s) are you working toward? ________________________________

  ____

- Does it still sound reasonable? ________________________________

  ____

- What systems or habits did you put into place to help you make progress? ______

  ____

- How did it go this week? ________________________________

  ____

- What things got in the way of progress this week? What things helped?__________

  ____

- Do you need prompts or reminders? If so, how and where? __________________

  ____

- What things do you want to celebrate about the process this week? _____________

  ____

- Do you need to change your habits? Do you need to change your goal?__________

  ____

- How can you support one another better next week? ____________________

  ____

DISCOVER YOUR FAITH

Remember when we talked about grace? Well, there are certain points in a Catholic person's life that are extra special, times when God's grace comes to us through real and visible events. These are known as the sacraments, and there are seven.

If you're a grown-up, you may have experienced some of these long ago without a thorough understanding. If you're a kiddo, you may have only been baptized. So, we're going to take a minute to review why these are important events.

The US Conference of Catholic Bishops (USCCB) website compares a sacrament to a hug that represents a parent's love for his or her child — it's a way to make an invisible reality (God's saving love and grace) visible:

> The saving words and deeds of Jesus Christ are the foundation of what he would communicate in the Sacraments through the ministers of the Church. Guided by the Holy Spirit, the Church recognizes the existence of Seven Sacraments instituted by the Lord. They are the Sacraments of Initiation (Baptism, Confirmation, the Eucharist), the Sacraments of Healing (Penance and the Anointing of the Sick), and the Sacraments at the Service of Communion (Marriage and Holy Orders). Through the Sacraments, God shares his holiness with us so that we, in turn, can make the world holier.[21]

If you visit this website, you can click on a description of each sacrament and learn where it came from in the Bible. Which ones have the members of your family experienced? What do you remember about those experiences? Did they help you understand or fulfill your mission in life?

Children can learn more by exploring the *Catholic Encyclopedia for Children* by Ann Ball. There are also books specific to Baptism and First Communion. This is a fun time to invite grandparents to describe how they felt when they experienced their own First Reconciliation and First Communion. (The scratchy clothes. The missing teeth. The happy hearts!)

ENCOURAGEMENT

If you just read about the Sacrament of Penance, then you know that the Church is full of people who mess up. In fact, we all do; it's part of being human.

Confessing your sins, asking for forgiveness, and receiving absolution wipes the slate clean, especially if you go and try to sin no more (particularly not in that specific way, and not intentionally). And that might be the most powerful motivator: the opportunity to start over and try, try again.

So, the next time someone on your family team makes a mistake, offer them the words of the great St. John Chrysostom, a Doctor of the Church and considered one of the greatest Christian preachers of all time. As he said about the salvation that Jesus' death and resurrection offers us sinners: "Let no one mourn that he has fallen again and again: for forgiveness has risen from the grave!"[22]

Try it! Reading aloud those formal words might just bring a smile to someone who's struggling after messing up. We've all fallen again and again, but we can be happy that Jesus rose from the dead so that we can be forgiven. It's an essential reminder of our ultimate hope, the whole reason *we* can rise up after we've fallen. Thank God!

PRAYER

Thanks, Jesus, for giving us real reminders of your grace in ways that our human brains can understand. Help us to do the same for others — to be great examples of your love! Amen.

TEAM SPIRIT

Close out your family meeting with some excitement and joy!

NOTES FOR NEXT TIME

____

____

WEEK 30

DATE ____________ TIME____________ PLACE ______________________________

OPENING RITUAL

Remember, parents, this is up to you and your creativity! Is it a song that you sing or listen to together? A "ready-set-go" team chant? A minute of jumping jacks to get out the wiggles? Try out some ways to make your meetings "official" and create a mood of openness and engagement.

PRAYER

Take sixty seconds to pray together. You can pray in silence, or you can recite a traditional prayer such as the Our Father or Hail Mary.

MISSION REVIEW

Ask someone to recite, write, or sing your family's mission statement.

VISION REVIEW

Read your vision statement aloud.

GOAL REVIEW

- What goal(s) are you working toward? ______________________________

  ____

- Does it still sound reasonable? ______________________________

  ____

- What systems or habits did you put into place to help you make progress? ________

  ____

- How did it go this week? ______________________________

  ____

- What things got in the way of progress this week? What things helped?__________

____

- Do you need prompts or reminders? If so, how and where? __________________

____

- What things do you want to celebrate about the process this week? _____________

____

- Do you need to change your habits? Do you need to change your goal? __________

____

- How can you support one another better next week? ________________________

____

DISCOVER YOUR FAITH

What do you want to be when you grow up? It's a question kids hear all the time. And the expected answer generally has to do with a job or career choice. But in the Catholic Church, it's more of a multi-part question. The Church identifies three main vocations, or states in life: single life, married life, and religious life.

This goes hand-in-hand with what we talked about when you were working on your family mission. Each person was uniquely made by God with talents and gifts that he calls us to use. Our vocation is the way God has called us to live while we use those unique talents and gifts.

In our culture, young people don't often think about certain vocations for themselves — the religious life, for example. But it's important to be able to understand what you might be hearing from God. And if you're already living a vocation, it's important to identify how you're serving God in that role.

If you first feel called to be single or married, then you might also choose a job or career. You might also decide to take part in lay ministries at your parish — volunteering to teach religious education, for example, or bringing the Eucharist to the sick.

If one feels called to the religious life, there are choices there, too. Men might sense a calling to be a priest, a deacon, or a religious brother. Women could be called to be a religious sister or a consecrated single woman living in the world. Some religious work in churches; some in hospitals or schools. Some might travel the world in service; some stay in their communities and work and pray without seeing outsiders.

Some people who choose a job or career and live as a single or married person decide later in life, after they retire or their spouse dies, to become a member of a religious community or take vows.

There are lots of ways to explore vocations. Maybe there's a religious congregation that's very active in your community, as the Oblate Sisters of Providence are in theirs (http://oblatesisters.com/). You can Google "catholic religious orders near me." Reach out to see how your family might get involved in their work.

You could go on a retreat as a family. While most parish retreats are structured for adult men or women, try Googling "Catholic family retreat" and your region. Or you could visit a Catholic shrine together — a great way to learn about some of the saints and leaders of the Faith, as well as to enjoy some gorgeous scenery (typically). Take a picnic!

Most importantly, give yourselves some time for discernment — a chance to listen to what God is saying and how he wants each of you to live out his plan for you. There are many, many ways to serve him. Rather than "What do you want to be when you grow up?" maybe the better question is, "How do you want to be when you grow up?"

ENCOURAGEMENT

You've spent quite a bit of time working on mission and vision statements. But author and inspirational speaker Simon Sinek prefers to focus on discovering what he calls a "Just Cause." It's a way of discovering your value by working on something bigger than yourselves, and it wraps mission and vision into one philosophy:

> A Just Cause is linked to our WHY, our noble purpose for being. Our WHY comes from our past — it is our origin story and it is who we are. Our Just Cause is our WHY projected into the future. It describes a future state in which our WHY has been realized. It is a forward looking statement that is so inspiring and compelling that people are willing to sacrifice to see that vision advanced. There are five criteria to have a Just Cause. It must be 1) for something, 2) inclusive, 3) service oriented, 4) resilient, and 5) idealistic.[23]

TALK IT OUT AND SEE IF YOU CAN IDENTIFY THE COMPELLING, INSPIRING REASON WHY YOU'RE WORKING TOGETHER — YOUR VERY OWN JUST CAUSE!

If your family is losing steam with your mission and vision, ask yourselves the bigger question: Why are you doing this exercise? It likely has something to do with growing closer to one another and to God, to living out his plan for your lives, because of the grace and love with which he has showered you. But talk it out and see if you can identify the compelling, inspiring reason why you're working together — your very own just cause!

PRAYER

Holy Spirit, please share with us your wisdom, so that we can hear your plan for us. And help guide us toward those noble things that are bigger than ourselves, whatever our vocation, so that we can be all that you created us to be.

TEAM SPIRIT

Close out your family meeting with some excitement and joy!

NOTES FOR NEXT TIME

WEEK 31

DATE ____________ TIME____________ PLACE ______________________________

OPENING RITUAL

Remember, parents, this is up to you and your creativity! Is it a song that you sing or listen to together? A "ready-set-go" team chant? A minute of jumping jacks to get out the wiggles? Try out some ways to make your meetings "official" and create a mood of openness and engagement.

PRAYER

Take sixty seconds to pray together. You can pray in silence, or you can recite a traditional prayer such as the Our Father or Hail Mary.

MISSION REVIEW

Ask someone to recite, write, or sing your family's mission statement.

VISION REVIEW

Read your vision statement aloud.

GOAL REVIEW

- What goal(s) are you working toward? ______________________________

  ____

- Does it still sound reasonable? ______________________________

  ____

- What systems or habits did you put into place to help you make progress? _______

  ____

- How did it go this week? ______________________________

  ____

- What things got in the way of progress this week? What things helped? ______________________________

- Do you need prompts or reminders? If so, how and where? ______________________________

- What things do you want to celebrate about the process this week? ______________________________

- Do you need to change your habits? Do you need to change your goal? ______________________________

- How can you support one another better next week? ______________________________

DISCOVER YOUR FAITH

If you've ever been in a non-Catholic church — say, evangelical, for example — you may have noticed a pretty huge difference in the décor.

Catholic churches are full of statues, stained-glass windows, crucifixes, and other ornamental pieces. Beyond being beautiful or even jaw-dropping, they serve a purpose. And no, it's not so that we can worship them, despite the rumors!

Many of the images in Catholic churches are like illustrations in a book — they tell the stories of the Bible. Some statues remind us of humans who lived incredible lives of worship and service; angels depict the glory of God in heaven; and statues of the Holy Family recall Jesus' Incarnation — his time here on earth. These images are designed to teach and inspire.

A Catholic Mass is designed to appeal to all of the senses, using music, bells, imagery, and on special occasions, incense. These elements can vary quite a lot from church to church. But the format is the same wherever you go, and it has been that way for centuries. There are always two main parts: the Liturgy of the Word and the Liturgy of the Eucharist.

If you look it up at merriam-webster.com, you'll see that the word "catholic" with a lowercase "c" means "comprehensive, universal." This is interesting, because the Catholic Faith with a big "C" is also universal. Catholicism is a religion shared by more than a billion people around the globe.

We also share a common liturgy. Every day, there are millions of people worshiping at the same time as you, all speaking and praying together in different parts of the world. It's a beautiful way to experience the lowercase "c" version of "communion," defined at merriam-webster.com as "an act or instance of sharing."

And it's an important way to maintain your relationship with Jesus — to meet him in prayer, and to celebrate his sacrifice for us.

"Can't we just pray at home?" If you've heard this from your kids (or even thought it yourself), then the booklet *Catholic Parent Know-How: Why Do We Have to Go to Mass* by Lorene Hanley Duquin (Huntington, IN: OSV, 2007) is a must-read. It's just eight pages, but it's packed with solid and specific reasoning, including answers to why you can't just pray at home.

ENCOURAGEMENT

Our household is a mishmash of styles when it comes to accomplishing our goals. I remain faithful to my FranklinCovey planner and a crisp pen for daily to-dos and planning. I prefer to work alone, and woe to those who get in my way.

But my significant other likes to write everything in his tablet with a stylus. His goals live more in his head, and he can even turn on the TV when he's tackling a task. My daughter, on the other hand, after trying a million productivity techniques, has come to rely on a system of online coworking, reminder apps, personal check-ins, and journaling.

If we three can have such wildly different styles and get along (most of the time), then there's room for your own family to seek the same goals but with different tools. Technology might be better for an alternative learner or savvy teen who would walk right past a sticky note on the door. Music or art might be another way to reach, inspire, remind, or motivate another. As you rally your team, leave looseness in the order for the diverse beauty with which God created you.

PRAYER

As you pray today, choose one of the ways identified in the USCCB's document called "Praying with Body, Mind, and Voice," available at https://www.usccb.org/prayer-and-worship/the-mass/upload/praying-with-body-mind-and-voice.pdf.

> Dear Jesus, thank you for giving us the example of the liturgy at the Last Supper. We are glad to share the Mass with Catholics around the world and spend time in your presence. Amen!

TEAM SPIRIT

Close out your family meeting with some excitement and joy!

NOTES FOR NEXT TIME

WEEK 32

DATE ____________ TIME______________ PLACE __________________________________

OPENING RITUAL

Remember, parents, this is up to you and your creativity! Is it a song that you sing or listen to together? A "ready-set-go" team chant? A minute of jumping jacks to get out the wiggles? Try out some ways to make your meetings "official" and create a mood of openness and engagement.

PRAYER

Take sixty seconds to pray together. You can pray in silence, or you can recite a traditional prayer such as the Our Father or Hail Mary.

MISSION REVIEW

Ask someone to recite, write, or sing your family's mission statement.

VISION REVIEW

Read your vision statement aloud.

GOAL REVIEW

- What goal(s) are you working toward? ____________________________________

  ____

- Does it still sound reasonable? ____

  ____

- What systems or habits did you put into place to help you make progress? _______

  ____

- How did it go this week? ____

  ____

- What things got in the way of progress this week? What things helped? ____________

  ____

- Do you need prompts or reminders? If so, how and where? ____________________

  ____

- What things do you want to celebrate about the process this week? ______________

  ____

- Do you need to change your habits? Do you need to change your goal? ___________

  ____

- How can you support one another better next week? _______________________

  ____

DISCOVER YOUR FAITH

Sometimes kids like to roll their eyes at the fourth commandment — "Honor your father and your mother" — especially when parents use it as a persuasive tool to get chores done. But there's *so much* meaning packed into this commandment, not just for how we should behave in our family, but also how we should behave in society.

The *Catechism of the Catholic Church* breaks it down.[24] It's more than we can cover in one sitting, but here's an example of how the Church extends its understanding of family:

> The fourth commandment *illuminates other relationships in society*. In our brothers and sisters we see the children of our parents; in our cousins, the descendants of our ancestors; in our fellow citizens, the children of our country; in the baptized, the children of our mother the Church; in every human person, a son or daughter of the One who wants to be called "our Father." In this way our relationships with our neighbors are recognized as personal in character. The neighbor is not a "unit" in the human collective; he is "someone" who by his known origins deserves particular attention and respect. (2212)

Later, the *Catechism* states:

> Becoming a disciple of Jesus means accepting the invitation to belong to *God's family*, to live in conformity with His way of life: "For whoever does the will of my Father in heaven

is my brother, and sister, and mother." (2233)

How does it change your idea of honoring your father and mother if we're all a part of God's family? As you learn as a family how to demonstrate God's love, understanding, and grace to one another, how do you extend that to your neighbors, the members of your parish, your fellow citizens, and everyone on this planet?

One organization that brings to life the ways in which we are responsible for our greater family is the Catholic Health Association of the United States (chausa.org). Their website says,

> In addition to providing health care services for those in need, Catholic health care providers are driven by the social teachings of the Catholic Church to act in ways that respect human dignity, pay special attention to the poor and vulnerable, steward resources, act on behalf of justice, and ensure the common good. These commitments often take health care providers beyond the walls of their facilities as they meet community needs, advocate for a just US health care system that works for everyone, and address more global health care concerns — such as human trafficking.

AS YOU LEARN AS A FAMILY HOW TO DEMONSTRATE GOD'S LOVE, UNDERSTANDING, AND GRACE TO ONE ANOTHER, HOW DO YOU EXTEND THAT TO YOUR NEIGHBORS, THE MEMBERS OF YOUR PARISH, YOUR FELLOW CITIZENS, AND EVERYONE ON THIS PLANET?

Other focus areas include diversity and disparities, the environment, ethics, global health, immigration, palliative care, and more.

You can find piles of activities, news, prayers, events, and learning tools in each of these focus areas on their website. Take a peek, and see which might help you toward your family's unique way of living out your faith!

ENCOURAGEMENT

Whenever you feel like your efforts toward your mission, vision, and goals are getting stale, pretend like you're telling someone about them for the first time.

Imagine meeting up with a friend you haven't seen in a while. When they ask what's new, describe to them what you've been working on. Share with them the most surprising things you've learned, the hardest and most rewarding things you've done.

Think about it for a bit and practice on one another. Or even better, go tell a long-lost friend. Their curiosity and interest are likely to reignite your enthusiasm and help you realize just how far you've come.

PRAYER

The time your family has spent together over the past few months has been designed to help you not only think about your faith but also live your faith.

Read this passage from 1 John 3:16–18, and take a moment to talk about what it means to each of you:

> By this we know love, that he laid down his life for us; and we ought to lay down our lives for the brethren. But if any one has the world's goods and sees his brother in need, yet closes his heart against him, how does God's love abide in him? Little children, let us not love in word or speech but in deed and in truth.

You might also enjoy listening to one of my favorite Catholic hymns, "Let There Be Peace on Earth," as performed by jazz great Harry Connick Jr. (available on YouTube). Or check out the version by Voices of Hope Children's Choir, also available on YouTube.

TEAM SPIRIT

Close out your family meeting with some excitement and joy!

NOTES FOR NEXT TIME

____

____

____

____

____

____

____

____

WEEK 33

DATE ____________ TIME____________ PLACE ______________________________

OPENING RITUAL

Remember, parents, this is up to you and your creativity! Is it a song that you sing or listen to together? A "ready-set-go" team chant? A minute of jumping jacks to get out the wiggles? Try out some ways to make your meetings "official" and create a mood of openness and engagement.

PRAYER

Take sixty seconds to pray together. You can pray in silence, or you can recite a traditional prayer such as the Our Father or Hail Mary.

MISSION REVIEW

Ask someone to recite, write, or sing your family's mission statement.

VISION REVIEW

Read your vision statement aloud.

GOAL REVIEW

- What goal(s) are you working toward? ________________________________

  ____

- Does it still sound reasonable? ____________________________________

  ____

- What systems or habits did you put into place to help you make progress? _______

  ____

- How did it go this week? ____

  ____

- What things got in the way of progress this week? What things helped?__________

____

- Do you need prompts or reminders? If so, how and where? __________________

____

- What things do you want to celebrate about the process this week? _____________

____

- Do you need to change your habits? Do you need to change your goal? __________

____

- How can you support one another better next week? ______________________

____

DISCOVER YOUR FAITH

The second great commandment — "You shall love your neighbor as yourself" — sounds like a very individual directive. And it is. In the end, each of us has to answer to God for how well we succeeded, or how badly we failed.

But the *Catechism* also explains how this should look in a family setting:

> The family should live in such a way that its members learn to care and take responsibility for the young, the old, the sick, the handicapped, and the poor. There are many families who are at times incapable of providing this help. It devolves then on other persons, other families, and, in a subsidiary way, society to provide for their needs: "Religion that is pure and undefiled before God and the Father is this: to visit orphans and widows in their affliction and to keep oneself unstained from the world." (2208)

That last line is straight from the Bible (James 1:27), so the Catholic Church isn't just making it up. And there are *many* such verses. Here are a few more:

> "He who is kind to the poor lends to the LORD, and he will repay him for his deed." (Proverbs 19:17)
>
> "In all things I have shown you that by so toiling one must help the weak, remembering the words of the Lord Jesus, how he said, 'It is more blessed to give than to receive.'" (Acts 20:35)

"Do not neglect to do good and to share what you have, for such sacrifices are pleasing to God." (Hebrews 13:16)

"He who has a bountiful eye will be blessed, for he shares his bread with the poor." (Proverbs 22:9)

I could go on, but it's pretty clear, right? Notice what's not said, however. God doesn't say, "Share only with the poor whom you know," or "Share with the poor whom you think deserve some of your bread."

There's no mention of helping only the weak who look like you, who live in your country, who seem to be working really hard. God is using "neighbor" broadly here. And we don't get to judge. The goal is to love like Jesus loves us — so much so that he died for our sins, so that we could be with him in heaven.

How does it look when your family lives out CCC 2208? Perhaps you have to nurture the idea first in your own family, among one another, then build from there. Maybe you're already doing all of this as a part of your goal. Is there still room to expand?

In a live broadcast on January 9, 2021, Pope Francis said, "Things will get better to the extent that, with God's help, we work together for the common good, putting the weakest and most disadvantaged at the center."[25] How does the common good look within your family, and how do you nurture it outside your home for others?

ENCOURAGEMENT

Motivational and organizational expert Simon Sinek believes that leadership requires a long view: "Everything about being a leader is like being a parent. It is about committing to the well-being of those in our care and having a willingness to make sacrifices to see their interests advanced so that they may carry our banner long after we are gone."[26]

This might help if you're working hard, but not seeing results right away. You may feed the hungry one week, and find a longer line of hungry people the next. The fact is, you're taking action for the good of others and keeping at it, without knowing yet how you're creating change. Stepping up is leadership.

It's also not limited to parents, even though they're the ones to typically get the ball rolling and provide the example in a family. "Leadership, true leadership, is not the bastion of those who sit at the top. It is the responsibility of anyone who belongs to the group," Sinek writes.[27]

After all, the goal of a leader, as well as a parent, is to teach those around you so well that you put yourself out of a job. The impacts of small steps today could move mountains tomorrow … or thirty years from now. A commitment to caring is the mark of a parent, a leader, or any person living God's commandment with the hope of heaven someday.

PRAYER

This week, as you talk about the idea of "neighbor," pray A Prayer to the Creator,[28] which Pope Francis included at the end of *Fratelli Tutti*, an encyclical letter he wrote in 2020:

Lord, Father of our human family,
you created all human beings equal in dignity:
pour forth into our hearts a fraternal spirit
and inspire in us a dream of renewed encounter,
dialogue, justice and peace.
Move us to create healthier societies
and a more dignified world,
a world without hunger, poverty, violence and war.
May our hearts be open
to all the peoples and nations of the earth.
May we recognize the goodness and beauty
that you have sown in each of us,
and thus forge bonds of unity, common projects,
and shared dreams. Amen.

Finally, find James 2:14–17 and read that passage. Sit quietly for a minute and listen to how God is speaking to you through those verses. Have a chat with God and one another. Ask God to show your family opportunities to love your neighbors as yourselves. Finish with a powerful amen!

TEAM SPIRIT

Close out your family meeting with some excitement and joy!

NOTES FOR NEXT TIME

WEEK 34

DATE ____________ TIME______________ PLACE __________________________________

OPENING RITUAL

Remember, parents, this is up to you and your creativity! Is it a song that you sing or listen to together? A "ready-set-go" team chant? A minute of jumping jacks to get out the wiggles? Try out some ways to make your meetings "official" and create a mood of openness and engagement.

PRAYER

Take sixty seconds to pray together. You can pray in silence, or you can recite a traditional prayer such as the Our Father or Hail Mary.

MISSION REVIEW

Ask someone to recite, write, or sing your family's mission statement.

VISION REVIEW

Read your vision statement aloud.

GOAL REVIEW

- What goal(s) are you working toward? ____________________________________

  ____

- Does it still sound reasonable? ____

  ____

- What systems or habits did you put into place to help you make progress? _______

  ____

- How did it go this week? ____

  ____

- What things got in the way of progress this week? What things helped?__________

____

- Do you need prompts or reminders? If so, how and where? __________________

____

- What things do you want to celebrate about the process this week? _____________

____

- Do you need to change your habits? Do you need to change your goal? __________

____

- How can you support one another better next week? ______________________

____

DISCOVER YOUR FAITH

I don't stay in one place very well. FOMO (fear of missing out) is real for me. As a kid, I'd stare longingly down the gravel country road on which we lived and wonder what was happening out there, in the world. Even at the tender age of ten, I was determined to move to a busy metropolis, to live in New York City when I grew up. I was kind of a weird kid.

So, I'm sharing this with myself as well as you. It's from the book I've mentioned before, *Renewing Catholic Family Life*, edited by Dr. Greg Popcak. In chapter 1, Dr. Timothy O'Malley talks about taking the time to appreciate the pretty incredible things happening right around us every day:

> As we bless our children, as we bless the food in our home, our travel to school, even blessing one another in our sorrows, we come to see the various ways that God can become present in our day-to-day life. We don't need transcendent experiences to perceive God's activity in our midst. We often need simply to attend to the signs that exist before our very eyes. Blessing invites us to slow down and attend to these signs. We learn to be grateful merely for the existence of the person in our presence, the one who is our mother, our father, or our child.[29]

At the same time, Dr. O'Malley isn't suggesting that we just sit around and look lovingly at one another. Rather, we are called to go beyond our immediate family and carry this sense of "God in our midst" from our homes out to people who are in need of it. We are called to offer the gift of our presence and love to everyone around us, regardless of whether we have race, class, region, religion, interest, or anything else in common:

> It is not enough for every individual family to experience affection for each other within the home. The domestic church must move beyond the walls of hearth and home to offer hospitality to the world. The charism of the family is to embody the sacramental love of the Word made flesh not in experiences of affinity, but in kinship offered to everyone who hungers and thirsts for meaning.[30]

GOD IS AT WORK IN THE BIG AND THE SMALL, AROUND THE GLOBE AND IN OUR LIVING ROOM. THIS IS WHERE WE'RE CALLED TO BE, AND WHERE WE'RE CALLED TO SEE HIM, TOO.

This call is a bit of yin and yang, which suits me especially well. Because after I've overbooked adventures to all the corners of the world, I'm ready to stay at home for a while and appreciate the easy way of being around people who know and love me. And because my travels typically aren't luxury trips, but are often to much poorer parts of the planet where I have little culturally in common, I come back with an ever deeper gratitude for the home and family that I have.

God is at work in the big and the small, around the globe and in our living room. This is where we're called to be, and where we're called to see him, too. As long as we're looking for him and heeding his call in all places, we're never missing out.

ENCOURAGEMENT

St. Teresa of Calcutta, more widely known as Mother Teresa, is known as the epitome of selflessness and faithful devotion. And it's a fair assessment to say that Saint Teresa gave everything — not just her life, but her genuine love — to the world's most unwanted: the poor suffering from leprosy, AIDS, and tuberculosis on the streets of Calcutta in India.

But did you know that this seemingly perfect saint suffered from what she called a "dark night of the soul" for fifty years? All that time she was doing God's work, she didn't directly feel God's presence. Saint Teresa didn't hear him when she prayed. She didn't have that awe of knowing that he was *there*.

That didn't stop her from radiating God's love. She continued to live out his initial call to her, to be like Jesus to those hurting in body, mind, and soul. Saint Teresa continued to smile through this period of uncertainty, so much so that no one realized what she was experiencing until much later. Even when she felt he was distant, she became God's ambassador to much of the globe.

It takes a massive amount of faith to continue with the kind of hands-on, in-the-gutter ministry that she ran, *especially* without a regular experience of God — to pray without sensing his comfort or hearing his direction, without hearing the Holy Spirit whisper through your heart and soul.

I'd like to say that if Saint Teresa can do it, anyone can. But maybe it's more accurate to say that if Saint Teresa could do so much with so little encouragement, we can at least plod on with our smaller good deeds, despite feeling occasionally uninspired.

Maybe she wasn't feeling it at the time, but I think we can all agree that Saint Teresa is enjoying the fullest glory of eternal life. And even when we aren't feeling it, we're still capable of doing *something* that shows our love for God and our neighbor and brings us closer to heaven. That's what faith is all about!

PRAYER

God, give us the strength and courage to offer hospitality to our families and to the world, as described by Saint Paul in his Letter to the Romans:

> May the God of steadfastness and encouragement grant you to live in such harmony with one another, in accord with Christ Jesus, that together you may with one voice glorify the God and Father of our Lord Jesus Christ. Welcome one another, therefore, as Christ has welcomed you, for the glory of God. (15:5–7)

TEAM SPIRIT

Close out your family meeting with some excitement and joy!

NOTES FOR NEXT TIME

WEEK 35

DATE ____________ TIME______________ PLACE __________________________________

OPENING RITUAL

Remember, parents, this is up to you and your creativity! Is it a song that you sing or listen to together? A "ready-set-go" team chant? A minute of jumping jacks to get out the wiggles? Try out some ways to make your meetings "official" and create a mood of openness and engagement.

PRAYER

Take sixty seconds to pray together. You can pray in silence, or you can recite a traditional prayer such as the Our Father or Hail Mary.

MISSION REVIEW

Ask someone to recite, write, or sing your family's mission statement.

VISION REVIEW

Read your vision statement aloud.

GOAL REVIEW

- What goal(s) are you working toward? ____________________________________

  ____

- Does it still sound reasonable?____

  ____

- What systems or habits did you put into place to help you make progress? _______

  ____

- How did it go this week? ____

  ____

- What things got in the way of progress this week? What things helped?__________

____

- Do you need prompts or reminders? If so, how and where? ____________________

____

- What things do you want to celebrate about the process this week? _____________

____

- Do you need to change your habits? Do you need to change your goal? __________

____

- How can you support one another better next week? ______________________

____

DISCOVER YOUR FAITH

We've all heard the old saying that it's not polite to talk about religion or politics, right?

But we're already talking about religion here. And Jesus was very much involved in the politics of his day. He was often challenging or being challenged by people in authority (see Mark 11:27–33 and Luke 20:1–8); in fact, Jesus was crucified for stirring up rebellion — a political punishment for a political crime.

We can't just put our faith to the side when the actions of a nation's leaders conflict with God's law. We're still called to obey the Ten Commandments, still required to love our neighbors as ourselves, and still obligated to live by the Beatitudes if we want to be followers of Christ.

This is *tough*. Even among Catholics, not everyone agrees on how this should look. We're all sinful, imperfect, and selfish sometimes. Even people with the best intentions can disagree, and love is too often in short supply. But that doesn't let us off the hook. As it says in Galatians 6:2, "Bear one another's burdens, and so fulfill the law of Christ."

Catholics have long taken their beliefs to government. When I was a girl in Catholic grade school, we learned all about Lech Walesa — a Catholic, a Nobel Peace Prize winner, and the founder of the Solidarity movement that toppled communism in Poland in 1989–90. Pope St. John Paul II's visits to his homeland and his meetings with Walesa lent inspiration and visibility to Walesa's efforts to protect workers' rights against government repression.

If your mission includes changing society in any way, there are faithful resources for study and action. The United States Conference of Catholic Bishops' Office of Justice, Peace and Human

Development has gathered many of these in a section of its website called "Forming Consciences for Faithful Citizenship."[31]

The US bishops emphasize that in the Catholic Tradition, responsible citizenship is a virtue, and participation in political life is a moral obligation. In the United States, voting is an especially important way to enact the social justice that is essential to Christian love, and "concerns the social, political and economic aspects and, above all, the structural dimension of problems and their respective solutions."[32]

Most importantly, don't forget that, for followers of Christ, humility, love, and prayers for wisdom and discernment are key elements of conversations about religion, politics, or any topic.

ENCOURAGEMENT

Motivational author and speaker Simon Sinek says, "When we have a clear sense of why we do what we do, we are better able to make decisions that steer our lives in ways that contribute directly toward our purpose, cause, or belief."[33]

This is why you did the hard work of writing a mission statement. Your family is figuring out why you're here, wonderfully created by God with special talents and gifts, and what is important to you. This helps you apply that filter we talked about earlier when you're faced with a decision about what to say or do, or not to say or do.

Keep using your mission, vision, and goals as tools to guide you. As time goes by, the process will become automatic, and your lives will feel more aligned with God's plan for you!

PRAYER

The First Letter of John says, "But if any one has the world's goods and sees his brother in need, yet closes his heart against him, how does God's love abide in him? Little children, let us not love in word or speech but in deed and in truth" (3:17–18).

Holy Spirit, show us how to love in deed and truth. Help us understand the best ways to do this, so that we can reflect Jesus' teachings in every part of our lives. Amen!

TEAM SPIRIT

Close out your family meeting with some excitement and joy!

NOTES FOR NEXT TIME

____

____

WEEK 36

DATE ____________ TIME______________ PLACE ______________________________

OPENING RITUAL

Remember, parents, this is up to you and your creativity! Is it a song that you sing or listen to together? A "ready-set-go" team chant? A minute of jumping jacks to get out the wiggles? Try out some ways to make your meetings "official" and create a mood of openness and engagement.

PRAYER

Take sixty seconds to pray together. You can pray in silence, or you can recite a traditional prayer such as the Our Father or Hail Mary.

MISSION REVIEW

Ask someone to recite, write, or sing your family's mission statement.

VISION REVIEW

Read your vision statement aloud.

GOAL REVIEW

- What goal(s) are you working toward? ______________________________

  ____

- Does it still sound reasonable?______________________________

  ____

- What systems or habits did you put into place to help you make progress? _______

  ____

- How did it go this week? ______________________________

  ____

- What things got in the way of progress this week? What things helped?__________

____

- Do you need prompts or reminders? If so, how and where? __________________

____

- What things do you want to celebrate about the process this week? _____________

____

- Do you need to change your habits? Do you need to change your goal? __________

____

- How can you support one another better next week? ____________________

____

DISCOVER YOUR FAITH

Pope Francis is a whiz at using modern, popular means of communicating an ancient message. Not only is he on Twitter, but the pope has also given two TED (Technology, Entertainment, Design) Talks.

His presentation at the TED2017 conference, called "The Future You: Why the Only Future Worth Building Includes Everyone," calls for a world where equality, solidarity, and tenderness are commonplace. Among his compelling and thought-provoking missives is this gem: "Good intentions and conventional formulas, so often used to appease our conscience, are not enough. Let us help each other, all together, to remember that the other is not a statistic or a number. The other has a face. The 'you' is always a real presence, a person to take care of."

This quote hit me in the gut. I am full of good intentions, and I can easily appease my conscience. Living in my bubble, I rarely meet the face of the other, even if I'm thinking of him or her all the time. But using real-world situations and accessible ways to deliver his message, Pope Francis has a gift for making the forgotten real.

I'd bet that there's a quote or two in this TED talk that resonates with your family. You can read the transcript of Pope Francis's talk at Time.com.[34] Or watch it with subtitles at Ted.com.[35]

Find your family's favorite quote, or choose a few that mean something to each of you. To bring home the message for little ones, the story of the Good Samaritan (Luke 10:25–37) is a concrete way to illustrate the concept of "other." Check out Tomie dePaola's book, *The Good Samaritan and Other Parables*.

TAKE A MOMENT TO THINK ABOUT WHO YOUR FAMILY'S "OTHER" MIGHT BE, AND HOW YOU MIGHT PUT A FACE TO THAT.

Take a moment to think about who your family's "other" might be, and how you might put a face to that. After all, as Pope Francis says, "A single individual is enough for hope to exist, and that individual can be you."

ENCOURAGEMENT

Shirley Young had a difficult start in life. She was a young Chinese girl living in the Philippines when the Japanese invaded. Her father was the consul general, so he was led away along with other officials, and they were later executed.

Meanwhile, all the wives and children of those officials moved in with Shirley and her mom and siblings — forty people in a home designed for one family. As the war slowly erased everyday necessities — water, electricity, shoes — everyone had to learn together to make and do for themselves.

Loss was a major part of her youth. And yet in that same situation, Shirley found a new kind of family, and hope. "The thing that I learned was that whatever the circumstance, you can be happy. Because actually, we had a very happy childhood," she said in an interview in 2003.[36]

After the war, Shirley and her family moved to America. She became a pioneering market research guru and was eventually hired by General Motors, where she worked her way up to a position as vice president. She ultimately led the company's effort to become the Chinese government's American partner in the auto industry … no small feat for anyone, but particularly astonishing for a woman, a Chinese person, and a survivor of war whose father was killed.

Are there circumstances that you or your family are overcoming right now? Is there a way you might be happy in them … or a way to even thrive? How might Shirley's story help someone you know, or someone whom you're trying to help?

PRAYER

This week, read Matthew 25:31–46, and think on the message for a bit. Then follow up with this prayer:

> O Holy Spirit, please open my eyes and help me to see God in the face of the other — the hungry, or the stranger — and give me the wisdom and courage to know how to respond.

TEAM SPIRIT

Close out your family meeting with some excitement and joy!

NOTES FOR NEXT TIME

WEEK 37

DATE ____________ TIME____________ PLACE ______________________________

OPENING RITUAL

Remember, parents, this is up to you and your creativity! Is it a song that you sing or listen to together? A "ready-set-go" team chant? A minute of jumping jacks to get out the wiggles? Try out some ways to make your meetings "official" and create a mood of openness and engagement.

PRAYER

Take sixty seconds to pray together. You can pray in silence, or you can recite a traditional prayer such as the Our Father or Hail Mary.

MISSION REVIEW

Ask someone to recite, write, or sing your family's mission statement.

VISION REVIEW

Read your vision statement aloud.

GOAL REVIEW

- What goal(s) are you working toward? ________________________________

  ____

- Does it still sound reasonable? ____________________________________

  ____

- What systems or habits did you put into place to help you make progress? ______

  ____

- How did it go this week? ____

  ____

- What things got in the way of progress this week? What things helped?__________

____

- Do you need prompts or reminders? If so, how and where? ____________________

____

- What things do you want to celebrate about the process this week? _____________

____

- Do you need to change your habits? Do you need to change your goal? __________

____

- How can you support one another better next week? _______________________

____

DISCOVER YOUR FAITH

How will you be the answer to someone's prayer?

We tend to do a lot of asking — asking other people for their prayers, and asking God for things in prayer. But it's exciting to imagine that we might actually be the very thing someone is praying for.

Sometimes the opportunities are obvious. You see a need (for food, or clothing, or an extra helping hand in the yard), and you fulfill it. Sometimes, however, you and your family might be an answer to someone's prayer simply by being family.

Pope Francis wrote a document called *Amoris Laetitia* (On Love in the Family, found online at Vatican.va). It's the length of a book, and it discusses modern families' current realities, how the Holy Family can serve as a model, the types of love, and ways the Church can minister to couples, children, and families.

Right at the start, Pope Francis makes it clear that he's not just talking to those perfect families that we all imagine when we picture a Catholic family: "This Exhortation … represents an invitation to Christian families to value the gifts of marriage and the family, and to persevere in a love strengthened by the virtues of generosity, commitment, fidelity and patience. Second, because it seeks to encourage everyone to be a sign of mercy and closeness wherever family life remains imperfect or lacks peace and joy."

When you have calm, courage, grace, or an extra measure of love to share, look to see who around you might be needing family. While there is a special bond within your immediate family, "we, though many, are one body in Christ, and individually members one of another" (Romans 12:5).

ENCOURAGEMENT

It's true — one of the fundamentals of a goal is the ability to measure it. Quantitatively. Business in particular loves ROI (return on investment).

But as a social media marketer, I often explain to clients that the things you *can* count — the number of likes, or the number of followers — are often meaningless to the bottom line. And the things that move the needle — sales growth, total revenue — are sometimes impossible to trace back to the six posts that someone saw on Facebook that made them go to the store and look for that loaf of bread. It's not like I can follow someone's eyeballs on that post and track them all the way to the supermarket checkout, ensuring that they weren't influenced by any friends or magazine ads or other promotions along the way to that purchase. (Though if Facebook could do that, they sure would.)

Author Herbert Lui wrote an eye-opening and insightful article on Medium called, "To Stick to Your New Year's Resolution, Get It Out of Your Head."[37] In it, he describes the idea of measuring inputs, not outputs — meaning, rather than focusing on the ends, look at your means. Are you doing your best? Are you really giving it your all? If so, then the results will follow. Rather than getting hung up on hitting your numbers, do your best work toward those goals and know that there will be progress regardless.

Along those lines, Lui advocates setting a standard of performance and building a system. These hearken back to our ground rules in chapter 4 (standard of performance) and Dr. Markman's guidance in week 9 on managing your environment (building a system). So, you didn't pray the Rosary every week last month? Fine. Did you pray the Rosary more often last month than you did last year? Great! Did you manage to respond with understanding and love when your six-year-old started throwing up right before it was time to pray the Rosary? Awesome! Did you put a rosary next to the TV remote so that you try to pray more often? Stellar.

In short: Try hard. Do better. Good things will come.

PRAYER

The Peace Prayer of Saint Francis is a fantastic reminder of how we can be the answer to someone's prayers. Although it wasn't actually written by Saint Francis, it reflects perfectly his devotion:

Lord, make me an instrument of Your peace;
Where there is hatred, let me sow love;
Where there is injury, pardon;
Where there is doubt, faith;
Where there is despair, hope;
Where there is darkness, light;

And where there is sadness, joy.
O Divine Master,
Grant that I may not so much seek
To be consoled as to console;
To be understood, as to understand;
To be loved, as to love;
For it is in giving that we receive,
It is in pardoning that we are pardoned,
And it is in dying that we are born to Eternal Life.
Amen.

TEAM SPIRIT

Close out your family meeting with some excitement and joy!

NOTES FOR NEXT TIME

WEEK 38

DATE ____________ TIME____________ PLACE ______________________________

OPENING RITUAL

Remember, parents, this is up to you and your creativity! Is it a song that you sing or listen to together? A "ready-set-go" team chant? A minute of jumping jacks to get out the wiggles? Try out some ways to make your meetings "official" and create a mood of openness and engagement.

PRAYER

Take sixty seconds to pray together. You can pray in silence, or you can recite a traditional prayer such as the Our Father or Hail Mary.

MISSION REVIEW

Ask someone to recite, write, or sing your family's mission statement.

VISION REVIEW

Read your vision statement aloud.

GOAL REVIEW

- What goal(s) are you working toward? ______________________________

  ____

- Does it still sound reasonable? ______________________________

  ____

- What systems or habits did you put into place to help you make progress? ______

  ____

- How did it go this week? ______________________________

  ____

- What things got in the way of progress this week? What things helped?__________

____

- Do you need prompts or reminders? If so, how and where? ____________________

____

- What things do you want to celebrate about the process this week? _____________

____

- Do you need to change your habits? Do you need to change your goal? __________

____

- How can you support one another better next week? ______________________

____

DISCOVER YOUR FAITH

Many activities end up pulling families in different directions — sports, lessons, theater, you name it. Add in playdates, sleepovers, girls' night out, guys' night out, work commitments, and homework, and the time that you actually spend together as a family slips away faster than our dog trying to avoid a bath.

So, it's extra special when you can all spend time doing something together … especially if that something benefits others and leaves you feeling like warm cookies inside.

> ***"BUT BE DOERS OF THE WORD, AND NOT HEARERS ONLY, DECEIVING YOURSELVES."*** **— JAMES 1:22**

Volunteering as a family is one of those things. Beyond the feel-good aspect, it's a calling. You can find many spots in the Bible where Jesus urges his followers to go and do. And Saint James urges us: "But be doers of the word, and not hearers only, deceiving yourselves" (1:22).

It's also important to being Catholic. Catholic social teaching urges us to give of our time and resources. The US Conference of Catholic Bishops lists seven themes of Catholic social teaching, which offer a us a nice blueprint for planning our volunteer efforts:

- Life and dignity of the human person
- Call to family, community, and participation

- Rights and responsibilities
- Option for the poor and vulnerable
- The dignity of work and the rights of workers
- Solidarity
- Care for God's creation

You can read much, much more about these on the USCCB website to see how they might influence or fit into your family's mission, vision, and goals.[38]

There are nonprofits that have put in the extra work to make volunteering as a family possible, even with little ones. Doing Good Together (doinggoodtogether.org) lists those kinds of opportunities. Even further, the organization's mission is "empowering families to raise caring, engaged children by offering unique programs and events, valuable services, and fun activities that promote kindness and giving." They have many suggestions to help parents do just that.

Create the Good (createthegood.aarp.org) is another such resource, but more specifically it allows you to search for volunteer events in your local area.

These can be a jumping-off point, too, for ideas that your family fleshes out on your own. Does your family go to the movies together often? Perhaps you can regularly invite a young person who wouldn't otherwise be able to go. Does your family go for a hike on Saturdays? Maybe you can take gloves and trash bags and clean up a parking lot or trail while you're there. Service is so much better when it's shared!

ENCOURAGEMENT

If you're trying to decide how you as a family might like to serve others, make sure you get everyone's input. Change expert Dr. John Kotter has written a lot about buy-in, and he knows that "choice motivates people to be far more committed to driving change than being told they have to do it."[39]

The Center on the Developing Child at Harvard University offers nine tips in their article, "How to Motivate Children: Science-Based Approaches for Parents, Caregivers, and Teachers."[40] Number six recommends giving children agency — letting them choose tasks, or have some say in how and when their tasks get done.

This might be useful not only for the kids in your family, but also the adults. Don't we all prefer to work on projects that mean something to us, on our own terms? If you feel like your great family adventure is hitting some roadblocks, consider alternative routes. Let someone else take the wheel for a while. Get out of the car and walk a distance. You get the idea! Helping map out the path to the destination is motivating for everyone involved.

It seems kind of obvious, right? We all like to shape our own destiny, or at least have a say in how our day is going to go. So, reflect on your family mission: What are your special interests, talents, and gifts? Think about your vision: How do you want the world to look because you used your talents and gifts? Think about your goals: How are you spending your time?

Make a list of possible volunteer activities, then choose *as a family*. You'll find that when your team says that yes, they want to do it, then they are much more willing to follow through — with enthusiasm. After all, they've already convinced themselves that this is a good idea!

PRAYER

The First Letter of Peter says, "As each has received a gift, employ it for one another, as good stewards of God's varied grace" (4:10).

> God, thank you for your grace. Please help us find the best way to use our gifts to help others, and bless all of our efforts. Amen!

TEAM SPIRIT

Close out your family meeting with some excitement and joy!

NOTES FOR NEXT TIME

____

____

____

____

____

____

____

____

WEEK 39

DATE ____________ TIME ____________ PLACE ____________________________

OPENING RITUAL

Remember, parents, this is up to you and your creativity! Is it a song that you sing or listen to together? A "ready-set-go" team chant? A minute of jumping jacks to get out the wiggles? Try out some ways to make your meetings "official" and create a mood of openness and engagement.

PRAYER

Take sixty seconds to pray together. You can pray in silence, or you can recite a traditional prayer such as the Our Father or Hail Mary.

MISSION REVIEW

Ask someone to recite, write, or sing your family's mission statement.

VISION REVIEW

Read your vision statement aloud.

GOAL REVIEW

- What goal(s) are you working toward? ________________________________

  ____

- Does it still sound reasonable? ____________________________________

  ____

- What systems or habits did you put into place to help you make progress? _______

  ____

- How did it go this week? ____

  ____

- What things got in the way of progress this week? What things helped?__________

____

- Do you need prompts or reminders? If so, how and where? __________________

____

- What things do you want to celebrate about the process this week? ____________

____

- Do you need to change your habits? Do you need to change your goal? __________

____

- How can you support one another better next week? ______________________

____

DISCOVER YOUR FAITH

We all know that racism is bad, right? But did you realize that it's a sin?

This is from "Open Wide Our Hearts: The Enduring Call to Love — A Pastoral Letter Against Racism," developed in November 2018 by the Committee on Cultural Diversity in the Church. A note: This is a long passage. This might be one that informs the adults, who can teach the kids. But it's pretty impactful all the way through, so I'm putting it here for you to digest in whatever way is most effective for you and your family:

> Racism can often be found in our hearts — in many cases placed there unwillingly or unknowingly by our upbringing and culture. As such, it can lead to thoughts and actions that we do not even see as racist, but nonetheless flow from the same prejudicial root. Consciously or subconsciously, this attitude of superiority can be seen in how certain groups of people are vilified, called criminals, or are perceived as being unable to contribute to society, even unworthy of its benefits. Racism can also be institutional, when practices or traditions are upheld that treat certain groups of people unjustly. The cumulative effects of personal sins of racism have led to social structures of injustice and violence that makes us all accomplices in racism. …
>
> As Christians, we are called to listen and know the stories of our brothers and sisters. We must create opportunities to hear, with open hearts, the tragic stories that are deeply imprinted on the lives of our brothers and sisters, if we are to be moved with

empathy to promote justice.[41]

Clear words on a hard topic, right?

Sometimes it feels like the Church is a stodgy old aunt stuck in the past. And then you read something like this and realize that she has wisdom for us right now, today, on relevant cultural topics. She addresses the nuances of this prickly subject, challenging even those of us who would never believe that we harbor a racist perspective, or who think that we haven't witnessed racism.

What are your takeaways from this? To listen to and accept as valid the experiences of others? To speak up, even when it's hard, even when it's your best friend making racist jokes? That it's a good thing our God is merciful, because humans have done a lot of bad things to other humans, and continue to do so? How might addressing racism fit into your family's vision?

St. Maximilian Kolbe, a Polish Conventual Franciscan Friar who helped hide Polish refugees from the Germans in World War II and spoke out against the Nazis, said, "The most deadly poison of our times is indifference. And this happens, although the praise of God should know no limits. Let us strive, therefore, to praise him to the greatest extent of our powers."

Saint Kolbe would be put to death for his caring. When he was sent to Auschwitz, he continued to pray openly and share his meager meals. He ultimately volunteered to die in place of a stranger.

The ways in which racism shows up has changed over the decades and centuries. But the Church is always striving to call out evil. And we're always called to do the same: to listen with open hearts and to promote justice.

ENCOURAGEMENT

Among Winston Churchill's many famous quotes is: "However beautiful the strategy, you should occasionally look at the results." In case you've ever wondered why I suggest that you walk through a Goal Review every week, this is why. Your family might be doing all kinds of awesome things: putting up posters around the house that list your goals, buying rosaries and saint books, or meeting once a week. (Ahem — you're meeting once a week, right?)

But if all of this is, to quote another great thinker (Shakespeare), "sound and fury, signifying nothing," then the effort isn't worth it. Remember when we talked about a growth mentality? It's one thing to try, fail, and learn from your mistakes. It's another to keep doing something that has zero results.

So, as you go through your Goal Review each week, be super honest. Because you don't get any points for spinning your wheels in the wrong direction, and because I won't even know whether you're actually successful or just exaggerating. If what you're doing isn't aligned with your mission and bringing your vision to life, then don't keep doing it. Change gears.

In fact, if your mission, vision, and goals aren't working for you, try something else. Only the Ten Commandments were carved in stone; you can start with a clean slate.

PRAYER

Holy Spirit, please fill me up with courage. The kind of courage I need to speak up and change hearts and systems that are racist. The kind of courage I need to admit that what I'm doing isn't working, and start over with something new. Most of all, the courage to do the good and right thing in every situation. Amen.

TEAM SPIRIT

Close out your family meeting with some excitement and joy!

NOTES FOR NEXT TIME

WEEK 40

DATE ____________ TIME____________ PLACE ______________________________

OPENING RITUAL

Remember, parents, this is up to you and your creativity! Is it a song that you sing or listen to together? A "ready-set-go" team chant? A minute of jumping jacks to get out the wiggles? Try out some ways to make your meetings "official" and create a mood of openness and engagement.

PRAYER

Take sixty seconds to pray together. You can pray in silence, or you can recite a traditional prayer such as the Our Father or Hail Mary.

MISSION REVIEW

Ask someone to recite, write, or sing your family's mission statement.

VISION REVIEW

Read your vision statement aloud.

GOAL REVIEW

- What goal(s) are you working toward? ________________________________

  ____

- Does it still sound reasonable?________________________________

  ____

- What systems or habits did you put into place to help you make progress? ______

  ____

- How did it go this week? ________________________________

  ____

- What things got in the way of progress this week? What things helped? __________

  ____

- Do you need prompts or reminders? If so, how and where? __________________

  ____

- What things do you want to celebrate about the process this week? ____________

  ____

- Do you need to change your habits? Do you need to change your goal? __________

  ____

- How can you support one another better next week? ______________________

  ____

DISCOVER YOUR FAITH

As we learned last week, the Church has always sought to address the issues of the day. Catholic social teaching explains why and how we should participate in these issues; as a family on a mission, you might appreciate knowing our faith's perspective, grounded in the Bible. I know that it helped me to be a better person of loving action!

The USCCB's letter "Open Wide Our Hearts" talks about specific things we've seen or experienced in the United States recently, and it explains how these are sins according to our faith:

> In recent times, we have seen bold expressions of racism by groups as well as individuals. The re-appearance of symbols of hatred, such as nooses and swastikas in public spaces, is a tragic indicator of rising racial and ethnic animus. All too often, Hispanics and African Americans, for example, face discrimination in hiring, housing, educational opportunities, and incarceration. Racial profiling frequently targets Hispanics for selective immigration enforcement practices, and African Americans, for suspected criminal activity. There is also the growing fear and harassment of persons from majority Muslim countries. Extreme nationalist ideologies are feeding the American public discourse with xenophobic rhetoric that instigates fear against foreigners, immigrants, and refugees. Finally, too often racism comes in the form of the sin of omission, when individuals, communities, and even churches remain silent and fail to act against racial injustice when it is encountered.[42]

Pretty direct, right? Perhaps more importantly, "Open Wide Our Hearts" explains how our country and we as citizens should do things differently to end these injustices and live according to God's word. The letter continues:

> Recall the words in the First Letter of John: "Everyone who hates his brother is a murderer, and you know that no murderer has eternal life remaining in him" (3:15). Racism shares in the same evil that moved Cain to kill his brother. It arises from suppressing the truth that his brother Abel was also created in the image of God, a human equal to himself. Every racist act — every such comment, every joke, every disparaging look as a reaction to the color of skin, ethnicity, or place of origin — is a failure to acknowledge another person as a brother or sister, created in the image of God. In these and in many other such acts, the sin of racism persists in our lives, in our country, and in our world.

OUR CATHOLIC FAITH IS READY TO HELP US IN THE GOOD AND THE BAD OF MODERN LIFE.

Our Catholic Faith is ready to help us in the good and the bad of modern life. The US Conference of Catholic Bishops is one great resource for a Catholic perspective on issues in the United States.

If addressing injustice is a part of your family's mission, check out the USCCB study guide for "Open Wide Our Hearts," available at usccb.org/resources/open-wide-our-hearts-study-guide.

And it can lead you to some family resources and more discussion:

- "A Process for Group Discernment," by We Are Salt and Light, https://www.wearesaltandlight.org/learn-together/process-group-discernment
- "Tip Sheet for Talking to Children About Racial Injustice and Protests," from Catholic Charities in the Archdiocese of Galveston-Houston, https://catholiccharities.org/wp-content/uploads/2020/06/2020-Counseling-Flyer-Tips-for-Kids-on-Racism-and-Protests.pdf
- "What Catholics Should Know About Raising White Kids," *US Catholic,* June 6, 2018, https://uscatholic.org/articles/201806/what-catholics-should-know-about-raising-white-kids/
- *ColorFull: Celebrating the Colors God Gave Us,* by Dorena Williamson (Nashville: B&H Publishing Group, 2018)
- "Resources for Racism in Our Streets and Structures: A Test of Faith, A Crisis for Our Nation," an entire list of articles, books, statements, videos, podcasts, and other resources compiled by the Georgetown University Initiative on Catholic Social Thought and Public Life and published June 5, 2020, at https://catholicsocialthought.georgetown.edu/essays/resources-for-racism-in-our-streets-and-structures-a-test-of-faith-a-crisis-for-our-nation

ENCOURAGEMENT

As life and business strategist Tony Robbins tweeted on July 11, 2017, "If you talk about it, it's a dream; if you envision it, it's possible; but if you schedule it, it's real."

You talked about the things you hope to achieve with your family when you went through the process of discovering your mission, right? And you envisioned them, too. Even better, you scheduled it all when you engaged in goal setting.

So, in essence, *it's real.* You're doing it. Not many people follow through on this kind of a change in their family and their faith. But here you are, in Week 40, making dreams happen.

PRAYER

Micah 6:8 is a beautiful passage about how we should be in the world. What does it mean for each of you? In your closing prayer this week, ask God for help to do the following:

> He has showed you, O man, what is good;
> and what does the LORD require of you
> but to do justice, and to love kindness,
> and to walk humbly with your God?

TEAM SPIRIT

Close out your family meeting with some excitement and joy!

NOTES FOR NEXT TIME

____

____

____

____

____

____

____

WEEK 41

DATE ____________ TIME ____________ PLACE ______________________________

OPENING RITUAL

Remember, parents, this is up to you and your creativity! Is it a song that you sing or listen to together? A "ready-set-go" team chant? A minute of jumping jacks to get out the wiggles? Try out some ways to make your meetings "official" and create a mood of openness and engagement.

PRAYER

Take sixty seconds to pray together. You can pray in silence, or you can recite a traditional prayer such as the Our Father or Hail Mary.

MISSION REVIEW

Ask someone to recite, write, or sing your family's mission statement.

VISION REVIEW

Read your vision statement aloud.

GOAL REVIEW

- What goal(s) are you working toward? ______________________________

  ____

- Does it still sound reasonable? ______________________________

  ____

- What systems or habits did you put into place to help you make progress? ________

  ____

- How did it go this week? ______________________________

  ____

- What things got in the way of progress this week? What things helped?__________

  ____

- Do you need prompts or reminders? If so, how and where? ________________

  ____

- What things do you want to celebrate about the process this week? ____________

  ____

- Do you need to change your habits? Do you need to change your goal?__________

  ____

- How can you support one another better next week? ____________________

  ____

DISCOVER YOUR FAITH

Immigration is one of those topics that people tend to form a strong opinion on without a deep understanding. And without first-hand experience or a law degree, it can be difficult to appreciate the immense challenges faced by immigrants and those seeking to improve the immigration system in the United States.

The good news is that there are ways to learn. The US Citizenship and Immigration Services agency, which administers the nation's immigration system, publishes our country's laws and policies online at https://www.uscis.gov/laws-and-policy. And organizations such as Casa de Paz in Denver, which shelters immigrants released from ICE until they can go home, offer a personal experience of families' struggles.

What does the Catholic Church say?

The Georgetown University Initiative on Catholic Social Thought and Public Life's blog from February 14, 2019, titled "Beyond the Wall: Human Impacts, Moral Principles, and Policy Directions on Immigration," is a great quick read for parents and older kids, if you want to go look it up.[43]

Bishops from the border regions of the United States and Mexico published a joint statement in April 2021 called "Situation at the US-Mexico Border," which can be found on the USCCB website. It's a short article — go check it out! It begins with this:

As US and Mexican bishops along the border, we witness daily the dilemma that our mi-

> grant sisters and brothers face. For most, the decision to migrate is not motivated by an indifference toward their homeland or the pursuit of economic prosperity; it is a matter of life or death. The situation is all the more difficult for children.
>
> Challenges such as these require humanitarian solutions. Undoubtedly, nations have the right to maintain their borders. This is vital to their sovereignty and self-determination. At the same time, there is a shared responsibility of all nations to preserve human life and provide for safe, orderly, and humane immigration, including the right to asylum.[44]

Pope Francis talks about immigrants quite a bit in *Fratelli Tutti* (On Fraternity and Social Friendship), the encyclical that he released on October 3, 2020. This document is all about brotherly love, without division. He says:

> If every human being possesses an inalienable dignity, if all people are my brothers and sisters, and if the world truly belongs to everyone, then it matters little whether my neighbour was born in my country or elsewhere. My own country also shares responsibility for his or her development, although it can fulfil that responsibility in a variety of ways. It can offer a generous welcome to those in urgent need, or work to improve living conditions in their native lands by refusing to exploit those countries or to drain them of natural resources, backing corrupt systems that hinder the dignified development of their peoples. (125)

As a mother, I try to imagine what I would do if I felt that my children were in danger — from gangs who extort and kill people in my neighborhood or recruit children with the threat of death; from hunger because there are no jobs; or because supply chains are broken in my country. I feel certain that I'd try to escape to protect or to feed them, and I'd keep going until I found somewhere safe.

I've also learned about the horrors that women and children often encounter as they migrate, and I wonder — would that be an acceptable risk, if death were the likely result of staying? I can only feel immense gratitude that I was born where I was, and empathy for those who were born into dangerous situations.

Kids can get their arms around this better with a book published jointly by the USCCB and Loyola Press called *Everyone Belongs*. It even includes printable worksheets for kids from kindergarten through grade 5.

Putting yourself in the shoes of immigrants is a good way to practice seeing Jesus in the other. Remember when we talked about different parts of the same body? God created each of us with special gifts and purposes, including our brothers and sisters born in other countries.

ENCOURAGEMENT

Even experts in goal setting and achievement can get behind the idea of negative goals. These aren't "bad" goals; they're goals for taking something away.

"Most people focus on what they need to add to their lives to get what they want. It might actually be what you're currently doing that's holding you back," says Gene Hammett in his article "You're Setting Goals All Wrong. Here's the Process You Should Be Using."[45]

He says that SMART goals (Remember those? They're specific, measurable, attainable, relevant, and time-bound) can actually be discouraging for some people. He encourages us to use a growth mindset — measuring *progress* as success. We talked about that earlier in this book when we learned about Carol Dweck.

Don't forget that you can change the stops (goals) on your journey to suit your family. Making a difference in your family and in the world isn't an instant process. In fact, if you're doing it right, you'll never be done. So, take away what isn't working, and keep adjusting until you find what does.

PRAYER

Lord, today we praise you with the words that we share with Catholics around the globe, in all kinds of languages:
Glory to God in the highest,
and on earth peace to people of good will. Amen.

TEAM SPIRIT

Close out your family meeting with some excitement and joy!

NOTES FOR NEXT TIME

WEEK 42

DATE ____________ TIME______________ PLACE ______________________________

OPENING RITUAL

Remember, parents, this is up to you and your creativity! Is it a song that you sing or listen to together? A "ready-set-go" team chant? A minute of jumping jacks to get out the wiggles? Try out some ways to make your meetings "official" and create a mood of openness and engagement.

PRAYER

Take sixty seconds to pray together. You can pray in silence, or you can recite a traditional prayer such as the Our Father or Hail Mary.

MISSION REVIEW

Ask someone to recite, write, or sing your family's mission statement.

VISION REVIEW

Read your vision statement aloud.

GOAL REVIEW

- What goal(s) are you working toward? ______________________________

  ____

- Does it still sound reasonable?______________________________________

  ____

- What systems or habits did you put into place to help you make progress? _______

  ____

- How did it go this week? ____

  ____

- What things got in the way of progress this week? What things helped?__________

____

- Do you need prompts or reminders? If so, how and where? ____________________

____

- What things do you want to celebrate about the process this week? _____________

____

- Do you need to change your habits? Do you need to change your goal? __________

____

- How can you support one another better next week? _______________________

____

DISCOVER YOUR FAITH

"You shall not oppress a stranger; you know the heart of a stranger, for you were strangers in the land of Egypt" (Exodus 23:9).

If you know the story of Exodus, you know the story of immigration. People have been fleeing oppression, danger, starvation, and slavery for centuries. Even the Bible has clear instructions on how we are to receive refugees: "When a stranger sojourns with you in your land, you shall not do him wrong. The stranger who sojourns with you shall be to you as the native among you, and you shall love him as yourself; for you were strangers in the land of Egypt: I am the Lord your God" (Leviticus 19:33–34).

"You shall allot it as an inheritance for yourselves and for the aliens who reside among you and have begotten children among you. They shall be to you as native-born sons of Israel; with you they shall be allotted an inheritance among the tribes of Israel. In whatever tribe the alien resides, there you shall assign him his inheritance, says the Lord God" (Ezekiel 47:22–23).

The Church has taken up this work as well — in the United States, specifically, Catholic Charities has made immigration one of its primary efforts. "Catholic Charities provides essential services to immigrants and newcomers to this country. CCUSA advocates for policies that protect family unity and allow newcomers an opportunity to contribute and participate more fully in our communities," its website states. "Catholic Charities affirms the inherent dignity bestowed on every human person, including immigrants and refugees, no matter the circumstances that compel a person to begin a new life in our community."

Has your family made it your mission to "love him as yourself"? Get involved in this effort! It's revealing to walk a mile in someone else's shoes, and to imagine what you might do if you and your family were in the same situation. There are Catholic Charities agencies in cities across the United States looking for help. Your local agency is a great place to enter the story.

> ***IT'S REVEALING TO WALK A MILE IN SOMEONE ELSE'S SHOES, AND TO IMAGINE WHAT YOU MIGHT DO IF YOU AND YOUR FAMILY WERE IN THE SAME SITUATION.***

ENCOURAGEMENT

"It is so easy to overestimate the importance of one defining moment and underestimate the value of making small improvements on a daily basis," writes James Clear, an expert on productivity and continuous improvement, in his book *Atomic Habits*.[46]

> Too often, we convince ourselves that massive success requires massive action. Whether it is losing weight, building a business, writing a book, winning a championship, or achieving any other goal, we put pressure on ourselves to make some earth-shattering improvement that everyone will talk about. Meanwhile, improving by one percent isn't particularly notable — sometimes it isn't even noticeable — but it can be far more meaningful, especially in the long run. The difference a tiny improvement can make over time is astounding.

What's he really saying here? Little changes add up, whether good or bad. So don't worry about making a giant improvement. Keep up those little changes — you'll get there!

PRAYER

Catholic Charities USA has a wealth of prayers and reflections on its website. Here's one for refugees and migrants:

> Merciful God, we pray for families and individuals who have left or fled their homes, seeking safer and better lives. We lift up to you their hopes, fears, and needs, that they may be protected on their journeys, their dignity and rights may be honored and upheld, and they may be welcomed with open arms into generous and compassionate communities. Amen.

TEAM SPIRIT

Close out your family meeting with some excitement and joy!

NOTES FOR NEXT TIME

WEEK 43

DATE ____________ TIME____________ PLACE ______________________________

OPENING RITUAL

Remember, parents, this is up to you and your creativity! Is it a song that you sing or listen to together? A "ready-set-go" team chant? A minute of jumping jacks to get out the wiggles? Try out some ways to make your meetings "official" and create a mood of openness and engagement.

PRAYER

Take sixty seconds to pray together. You can pray in silence, or you can recite a traditional prayer such as the Our Father or Hail Mary.

MISSION REVIEW

Ask someone to recite, write, or sing your family's mission statement.

VISION REVIEW

Read your vision statement aloud.

GOAL REVIEW

- What goal(s) are you working toward? ________________________________

  ____
- Does it still sound reasonable?______________________________________

  ____
- What systems or habits did you put into place to help you make progress? _______

  ____
- How did it go this week? ____

  ____

- What things got in the way of progress this week? What things helped?__________

  ____

- Do you need prompts or reminders? If so, how and where? ____________________

  ____

- What things do you want to celebrate about the process this week? _____________

  ____

- Do you need to change your habits? Do you need to change your goal? __________

  ____

- How can you support one another better next week? _______________________

  ____

DISCOVER YOUR FAITH

Are you a family who loves to be outdoors? Pope Francis is really passionate about caring for "our common home," as he calls our planet. All of us are affected by decisions that impact the earth, whether they're made in our city or around the globe … and the most vulnerable among us are often much more affected than others. Pope Francis shows us how caring for the environment is connected to the responsibility God gave us to take care of his creation.

In 2015, Pope Francis wrote a beautiful encyclical — an open letter to the whole Church — on living in harmony with nature and our fellow human beings. It's called *Laudato Sí* (On the Care of Our Common Home), and you can find it online at Vatican.va. OSV also published a collection of Pope Francis's writings about the environment called *Our Mother Earth: A Christian Reading of the Challenge of the Environment.*

There's an online resource too for families and parishes who want to know how to make a difference. Catholic Climate Covenant is an organization that can help you discover ways to live out your faith by being good stewards of creation.

A little background for the grown-ups and big kids:

> In 2006, to address growing ecological awareness and the need to implement Catholic social teaching on ecology within the US Church, the United States Conference of Catholic Bishops (USCCB) helped form Catholic Climate Covenant. Inspired by the USCCB's 2001 statement on climate change, and supported by nineteen national partners …

> Catholic Climate Covenant helps US Catholics respond to the Church's call to care for creation and care for the poor.
>
> We are grounded in the Church's deep history of teaching on creation, ecology, and the poor. Caring for creation and caring for the poor have been a part of the Catholic story since the beginning, but in recent years St. John Paul II, Pope Emeritus Benedict XVI, and especially Pope Francis have added a sense of urgency to their call for Catholics to act on climate change. The US Bishops themselves having been calling for action since 1981.[47]

Before you think this is too big for you to tackle, consider how this work starts with your little team at home:

> In the family we first learn how to show love and respect for life; we are taught the proper use of things, order and cleanliness, respect for the local ecosystem, and care for all creatures. In the family we receive an integral education, which enables us to grow harmoniously in personal maturity. In the family we learn to ask without demanding, to say "thank you" as an expression of genuine gratitude for what we have been given, to control our aggressivity and greed, and to ask forgiveness when we have caused harm. These simple gestures of heartfelt courtesy help to create a culture of shared life and respect for our surroundings.[48]

If caring for the Earth is a part of your family's mission and vision, you might find some exciting ideas on the Catholic Climate Covenant website, or in the pope's writings. And you may enjoy the short video under Resources/Videos about the cool things kids are doing to change the planet, called "I'm Only a Kid, I Can't Do Anything About Climate Change … Right?"

ENCOURAGEMENT

Even little ones can feel inspired by NASA's Dr. Ellen Ochoa, an inventor, astronaut, former director of the Johnson Space Center, and the first Latina woman in space, who said, "You don't have to wait until you're older to really make an impact on other people's lives."

In a "Women in Innovation" video from April 23, 2018, by the United States Patent and Trademark Office, Dr. Ochoa describes how she was captivated as a little girl by the Apollo space program, even though at that time, no one would have encouraged a little girl to think about becoming an astronaut. But as she rose to the top of her field, Dr. Ochoa was inspired by the women ahead of her who did things no one ever thought they could do. And she's seen young people serve as mentors and an inspiration to others of all ages.

So don't ever believe that because you're one person, or one family, or that you're "just a kid," you can't make a difference. As Dr. Ochoa says, "Just dream bigger dreams. Have bigger goals!"[49] (You can find the video on YouTube. It's less than five minutes long — take a look!)

PRAYER

Jesus really believes in the power of kids. In fact, in Luke 18:16, he says, "Let the children come to me, and do not hinder them; for to such belongs the kingdom of God." God, Father, Son, and Holy Spirit, help us to remember how powerful we are with your help. Allow us to keep making a difference on this earth. Amen!

TEAM SPIRIT

Close out your family meeting with some excitement and joy!

NOTES FOR NEXT TIME

____

____

____

____

____

____

____

____

WEEK 44

DATE ____________ TIME____________ PLACE ______________________________

OPENING RITUAL

Remember, parents, this is up to you and your creativity! Is it a song that you sing or listen to together? A "ready-set-go" team chant? A minute of jumping jacks to get out the wiggles? Try out some ways to make your meetings "official" and create a mood of openness and engagement.

PRAYER

Take sixty seconds to pray together. You can pray in silence, or you can recite a traditional prayer such as the Our Father or Hail Mary.

MISSION REVIEW

Ask someone to recite, write, or sing your family's mission statement.

VISION REVIEW

Read your vision statement aloud.

GOAL REVIEW

- What goal(s) are you working toward? ______________________________

  ____

- Does it still sound reasonable? ______________________________

  ____

- What systems or habits did you put into place to help you make progress? _______

  ____

- How did it go this week? ______________________________

  ____

- What things got in the way of progress this week? What things helped? ______________________

  ____

- Do you need prompts or reminders? If so, how and where? ______________________

  ____

- What things do you want to celebrate about the process this week? ______________________

  ____

- Do you need to change your habits? Do you need to change your goal? ______________________

  ____

- How can you support one another better next week? ______________________

  ____

DISCOVER YOUR FAITH

Some people like to dismiss environmental causes with the argument "people first." But as the Catholic Church explains, there's no way to separate care for people and care for the environment.

In *Caritas in Veritate* (On Integral Human Development in Charity and Truth), Pope Emeritus Benedict XVI says: "The book of nature is one and indivisible. … Our duties towards the environment are linked to our duties towards the human person, considered in himself and in relation to others."[50]

In fact, Pope Benedict urges a rethinking of our relationship with the environment. Read paragraphs 48 to 51 of this document. You can read ahead of time and then share the important points with your children, or read aloud as a family, either in one sitting or over the course of a few days. You'll discover some remarkable and beautiful teachings about how people should interact with one another and God's creation.

AS THE CATHOLIC CHURCH EXPLAINS, THERE'S NO WAY TO SEPARATE CARE FOR PEOPLE AND CARE FOR THE ENVIRONMENT.

And then there is *Laudato Sí* (On Care for Our Common Home), Pope Francis's loving and urgent call for humanity to face the impact of our actions on both the environment and one another. In this encyclical, released May 24, 2015, the pontiff eloquently iterates the ways in which our responsibility toward our fellow humans and toward the environment are inextricably linked:

> Climate change is a global problem with grave implications: environmental, social, economic, political and for the distribution of goods. It represents one of the principal challenges facing humanity in our day. Its worst impact will probably be felt by developing countries in coming decades. … Sadly, there is widespread indifference to such suffering, which is even now taking place throughout our world. Our lack of response to these tragedies involving our brothers and sisters points to the loss of that sense of responsibility for our fellow men and women upon which all civil society is founded.

There are also resources for grown-ups on simplifying your home and aligning your choices with the values of solidarity and sustainability.

You can also spend some time learning about St. Francis of Assisi, whose name Pope Francis chose in honor of the patron saint of animals and ecology. Saint Francis's feast day is October 4, a great day to celebrate the season of harvest and abundance from our big, beautiful planet.

ENCOURAGEMENT

Busy, busy, busy. When you're raising kids, working and caring for your home, trying to be a good member of your community, and learning about your faith, it sometimes feels like you're on a hamster wheel, just running in place. Or on a treadmill set to "high." Pause too long, and you'll be flung right off.

Trust that things will get easier. This too shall pass. Kids grow up. You gain wisdom and experience. The pace of change slows. It might seem breathless right now, but soon, every now and then, you'll catch your breath. Trust Ecclesiastes 3:1–8:

> For everything there is a season, and a time for every matter under heaven:
> a time to be born, and a time to die;
> a time to plant, and a time to pluck up what is planted;
> a time to kill, and a time to heal;
> a time to break down, and a time to build up;
> a time to weep, and a time to laugh;
> a time to mourn, and a time to dance;
> a time to cast away stones, and a time to gather stones together;
> a time to embrace, and a time to refrain from embracing;
> a time to seek, and a time to lose;
> a time to keep, and a time to cast away;
> a time to tear, and a time to sew;
> a time to keep silence, and a time to speak;
> a time to love, and a time to hate;
> a time for war, and a time for peace.

PRAYER

These prayers of petition are from the USCCB's web page, under "Prayers on the Care of Creation." You can read them together, or you can take turns reading the petitions, all responding together with "Lord, hear our prayer."

O Lord, grant us the grace to respect and care for Your creation.
Lord, hear our prayer.
O Lord, bless all of your creatures as a sign of Your wondrous love.
Lord, hear our prayer.
O Lord, help us to end the suffering of the poor and bring healing to all of your creation.
Lord, hear our prayer.
O Lord, help us to use our technological inventiveness to undo the damage we have done to Your creation and to sustain Your gift of nature.
Lord, hear our prayer.

TEAM SPIRIT

Close out your family meeting with some excitement and joy!

NOTES FOR NEXT TIME

____

____

____

____

____

____

____

____

WEEK 45

DATE ____________ TIME_____________ PLACE _________________________________

OPENING RITUAL

Remember, parents, this is up to you and your creativity! Is it a song that you sing or listen to together? A "ready-set-go" team chant? A minute of jumping jacks to get out the wiggles? Try out some ways to make your meetings "official" and create a mood of openness and engagement.

PRAYER

Take sixty seconds to pray together. You can pray in silence, or you can recite a traditional prayer such as the Our Father or Hail Mary.

MISSION REVIEW

Ask someone to recite, write, or sing your family's mission statement.

VISION REVIEW

Read your vision statement aloud.

GOAL REVIEW

- What goal(s) are you working toward? ____________________________________

  ____

- Does it still sound reasonable?____

  ____

- What systems or habits did you put into place to help you make progress? _______

  ____

- How did it go this week? ____

  ____

- What things got in the way of progress this week? What things helped?__________

  ____

- Do you need prompts or reminders? If so, how and where? ____________________

  ____

- What things do you want to celebrate about the process this week? ______________

  ____

- Do you need to change your habits? Do you need to change your goal? __________

  ____

- How can you support one another better next week? ________________________

  ____

DISCOVER YOUR FAITH

Have you ever heard of St. Kateri Tekakwitha?

She was the first Native American to be named a saint by the Catholic Church. Also known as the Lily of the Mohawks, she is the patron saint of ecology and the environment.

Honoring indigenous people around the world and their connection with God's creation is a Catholic endeavor embraced by Pope Francis, who took the name Francis in honor of Saint Francis of Assisi, the patron saint of animals and ecology. Pope Francis's encyclical *Laudato Sí* opens with a quote from Saint Francis: "Praise be to you, my Lord, through our Sister, Mother Earth, who sustains and governs us, and who produces various fruit with coloured flowers and herbs."

Later in this great work, Pope Francis speaks directly about Native Americans and indigenous people:

> It is essential to show special care for indigenous communities and their cultural traditions. They are not merely one minority among others, but should be the principal dialogue partners, especially when large projects affecting their land are proposed. For them, land is not a commodity but rather a gift from God and from their ancestors who rest there, a sacred space with which they need to interact if they are to maintain their identity and values. When they remain on their land, they themselves care for it best.[51]

There are many ways for your family to be supportive of this effort. The Saint Kateri Conservation

Center (kateri.org) is a super cool resource for ideas, including how to create a Saint Kateri habitat at home. See the menu under "To Help."

Saint Kateri is also the inspiration for a ministry at St. Benedict Parish in Chicago serving Native American Catholics. An article in *US Catholic* by journalist Judith Valente describes some of the ways in which the Church is attempting to atone for the sins of the faithful against the indigenous people and how, specifically, the Saint Kateri Center seeks to help Catholic Native people in the area integrate their culture and their faith.[52]

Today, there's greater recognition of similarities between Native and Catholic practices, and appreciation for the beautiful differences with which God created all of his people. Yet it's a small step among many bigger steps that still need to take place. After all, the story of Saint Kateri is one of "a woman forced to relinquish her family, tribe, and Native spiritual traditions to follow the Catholic faith," Valente notes.

To learn more about this beloved saint, adults might like to check out *Saint Kateri: Lily of the Mohawks* by Matthew and Margaret Bunson. And for little ones, the Tiny Saints® board book *You Do Not Need to Worry* from OSV tells the story of the saint in the context of Matthew 6.

Saint Kateri is just one example of people who are not white, who are not from Europe, but who have gone on to become saints in the Catholic Church. Sainthood is open to us all! And her story is a reminder that we always need to see Jesus in the other, regardless of how different someone might seem. The Catholic Church may be working on this, but the biggest effect on hearts happens right in our homes.

ENCOURAGEMENT

There's a Chinese proverb that says, "The best time to plant a tree was twenty years ago. The next best time is now."

While literally planting trees is definitely in keeping with our call as Catholics to care for creation, the phrase is also a great reminder that even if we haven't been doing all the things we should over the years (or over the past forty-four weeks) to develop our relationship with God and our family, it's never too late to start.

In fact, now is exactly the time to start. Change may be slow. You may feel like spindly saplings blowing in the breeze for a long time. But putting off starting is only delaying that day, twenty years out, when you can look around and see the incredible growth of those seeds that you planted with love and hope.

PRAYER

This week, end with this prayer:

Prayer to the Lily of the Mohawks

Blessed Kateri, you are revered as the mystic of the American wilderness.
Though orphaned at the age of four,
and left with a scarred face and

damaged eyesight from illness,
you were esteemed among the Mohawk tribe.
When you asked to be baptized a Christian
you subjected yourself
to abuse by your people
and were forced to run away.
You endured many trials but
still flowered in prayer and holiness,
dedicating yourself totally to Christ.
I ask you to be my spiritual guide
along my journey through life.
Through your intercession,
I pray that I may always be
loyal to my faith in all things.
Amen.

TEAM SPIRIT

Close out your family meeting with some excitement and joy!

NOTES FOR NEXT TIME

____

____

____

____

____

____

____

____

WEEK 46

DATE ____________ TIME____________ PLACE ______________________________

OPENING RITUAL

Remember, parents, this is up to you and your creativity! Is it a song that you sing or listen to together? A "ready-set-go" team chant? A minute of jumping jacks to get out the wiggles? Try out some ways to make your meetings "official" and create a mood of openness and engagement.

PRAYER

Take sixty seconds to pray together. You can pray in silence, or you can recite a traditional prayer such as the Our Father or Hail Mary.

MISSION REVIEW

Ask someone to recite, write, or sing your family's mission statement.

VISION REVIEW

Read your vision statement aloud.

GOAL REVIEW

- What goal(s) are you working toward? ______________________________

  ____

- Does it still sound reasonable? ______________________________

  ____

- What systems or habits did you put into place to help you make progress? ________

  ____

- How did it go this week? ______________________________

  ____

- What things got in the way of progress this week? What things helped?__________

____

- Do you need prompts or reminders? If so, how and where? __________________

____

- What things do you want to celebrate about the process this week? _____________

____

- Do you need to change your habits? Do you need to change your goal? __________

____

- How can you support one another better next week? _______________________

____

DISCOVER YOUR FAITH

One of my neighbors just so happens to be a deacon in a Catholic parish not too far from us that offers services for the deaf, including Mass with ASL.

This led me to discover an organization devoted to encouraging participation in the Catholic Church by those living with a whole range of different abilities. The National Catholic Partnership on Disability (ncpd.org) has a wealth of resources for those with autism spectrum disorder, blindness or vision loss, deafness or hearing loss, intellectual and developmental disabilities, mental illness, and physical disability.

HOW MIGHT YOUR FAMILY MAKE YOUR PARISH MORE WELCOMING TO THOSE OF DIFFERENT ABILITIES? HOW MIGHT YOU MAKE YOUR HOME AND YOUR LIVES MORE WELCOMING?

Such assets as plans for a sensory-friendly Mass seem to strongly reflect Pope Francis's guidance that "inclusion should be the 'rock' on which to build programmes and initiatives of civil institutions meant to ensure that no one, especially those in greatest difficulty, is left behind. The strength of a chain depends upon the attention paid to its weakest links."[53]

Investigating the blogs, webinars, and links at the National Catholic Partnership on Disability website reinforced for me how much I take for granted, and helped me realize ways I could be more inclusive, particularly for the "invisible" disorders that are sometimes only revealed through personal relationship.

How might your family make your parish more welcoming to those of different abilities? How might you make your home and your lives more welcoming? After all, as Pope Francis says, "frailty is part of everyone's life."

We all have strengths and challenges and depend on the varying abilities and grace of others to truly flourish. At the beginning of this year, each member of your family identified your unique strengths. How can you interlock your strengths with others' challenges, and find others who have strengths where you have challenges, so that you all can truly reflect the body of Christ?

Remember Romans 15:5–6: "May the God of steadfastness and encouragement grant you to live in such harmony with one another, in accord with Christ Jesus, that together you may with one voice glorify the God and Father of our Lord Jesus Christ."

ENCOURAGEMENT

If your goals include one particularly daunting task, just try eating the frog.

(Not literally, of course! Stay with me here …)

Mark Twain once said that if your job is to eat a live frog, it's best to do it first thing in the morning. Then you can feel pretty confident that there will be nothing worse all day.

Of course, he wasn't suggesting that you actually eat a live frog. Nor am I. And it does sound worse than anything else I've done today. Instead, "eat the frog" has come to mean getting the worst thing done first. Rather than putting off the dreaded task and feeling hounded by it all day (or week or month), jump in right away and knock it out. Everything that comes later is just gravy. Which is so much tastier than live frogs!

PRAYER

As Jesus told us in Matthew 11:5, "The blind receive their sight and the lame walk, lepers are cleansed and the deaf hear, and the dead are raised up, and the poor have good news preached to them." Thank you, Jesus, for blessing us with and healing our frailties, seen and unseen, and giving us hope to be made whole in heaven. Amen.

TEAM SPIRIT

Close out your family meeting with some excitement and joy!

NOTES FOR NEXT TIME

____

____

WEEK 47

DATE ____________ TIME____________ PLACE ______________________________

OPENING RITUAL

Remember, parents, this is up to you and your creativity! Is it a song that you sing or listen to together? A "ready-set-go" team chant? A minute of jumping jacks to get out the wiggles? Try out some ways to make your meetings "official" and create a mood of openness and engagement.

PRAYER

Take sixty seconds to pray together. You can pray in silence, or you can recite a traditional prayer such as the Our Father or Hail Mary.

MISSION REVIEW

Ask someone to recite, write, or sing your family's mission statement.

VISION REVIEW

Read your vision statement aloud.

GOAL REVIEW

- What goal(s) are you working toward? ________________________________

  ____

- Does it still sound reasonable? ________________________________

  ____

- What systems or habits did you put into place to help you make progress? ______

  ____

- How did it go this week? ________________________________

  ____

- What things got in the way of progress this week? What things helped?__________

  ____

- Do you need prompts or reminders? If so, how and where? __________________

  ____

- What things do you want to celebrate about the process this week? _____________

  ____

- Do you need to change your habits? Do you need to change your goal? __________

  ____

- How can you support one another better next week? _______________________

  ____

DISCOVER YOUR FAITH

You may have your mother's eyes, or your dad's chin. Maybe you have red hair like one of your grandparents. But no matter what you look like, you were made by God "in his own image" (Genesis 1:27).

God created us. As it says in the Book of Psalms, "Thou didst knit me together in my mother's womb" (139:13). And because of this, every life has dignity — every life is worthy of honor and respect — from start to finish, no matter what.

This belief is foundational to the Catholic Faith, as the USCCB explains on its webpage entitled "Life and Dignity of the Human Person" (https://www.usccb.org/beliefs-and-teachings/what-we-believe/catholic-social-teaching/life-and-dignity-of-the-human-person). Pope Francis helps us understand what that means in today's society:

> Our defense of the innocent unborn, for example, needs to be clear, firm and passionate, for at stake is the dignity of a human life, which is always sacred and demands love for each person, regardless of his or her stage of development. Equally sacred, however, are the lives of the poor, those already born, the destitute, the abandoned and the underprivileged, the vulnerable infirm and elderly exposed to covert euthanasia, the victims of human trafficking, new forms of slavery, and every form of rejection.[54]

Over the past few weeks, we've talked about ways to respect life, even when there are differences.

Because where we might see differences, God sees his children, all created in his likeness. "Differences of color, religion, talent, place of birth or residence, and so many others," Pope Francis says, "cannot be used to justify the privileges of some over the rights of all."[55]

One very beautiful way for your family to show respect for the lives of those whom God has created is to volunteer with or donate to the Christ Child Society. This nationwide organization fosters an active love for all life starting with layettes for pregnant mothers and including efforts to serve children in poverty or in need of resources.

If there's a chapter near you, you can help in a hands-on way by preparing the layettes for new mothers, sorting winter coats for kids, or helping out with a book drive. If there's not a chapter near you, you can begin one, or you can donate online. The Christ Child website, https://www.nationalchristchild.org/, has details.

Other opportunities to partner with an organization's efforts include getting involved with your local Catholic Charities branch, or joining (or starting) Walking With Moms in Need at your parish. Visit https://www.walkingwithmoms.com/ to learn more.

As the US Conference of Catholic Bishops' website points out, every person is precious, from the moment God formed us until he calls us to be with him again.

ENCOURAGEMENT

Changing the world can sometimes feel like trying to eat every one of the flavors in Baskin Robbins' lineup in one sitting: idealistic, but impossible. So instead, start with what you can do, and what you can change, whether that's in your home, your neighborhood, or maybe your country.

Consider the example of St. Maria de Jesus Sacramentado, who "lived a simple life, unmarked by miraculous or extraordinary events," according to her biography on the website for the Community Saint Maria de Jesus Sacramentado in Phoenix. Yet her work as a nurse, caring for the poor and the sick, changed the lives of those for whom she cared.

Bring it back to your mission, where you identified what your family cares about. Keep that front and center; passion can be a powerful source of persistence.

PRAYER

We read in 1 Corinthians 3:16, "Do you not know that you are God's temple and that God's Spirit dwells in you? If any one destroys God's temple, God will destroy him. For God's temple is holy, and that temple you are." God, we're grateful for the gift of our lives each and every day. Help us to see your Spirit within the people around us, and give us courage to defend the holiness of life in every way. Amen.

TEAM SPIRIT

Close out your family meeting with some excitement and joy!

NOTES FOR NEXT TIME

WEEK 48

DATE ____________ TIME______________ PLACE __________________________________

OPENING RITUAL

Remember, parents, this is up to you and your creativity! Is it a song that you sing or listen to together? A "ready-set-go" team chant? A minute of jumping jacks to get out the wiggles? Try out some ways to make your meetings "official" and create a mood of openness and engagement.

PRAYER

Take sixty seconds to pray together. You can pray in silence, or you can recite a traditional prayer such as the Our Father or Hail Mary.

MISSION REVIEW

Ask someone to recite, write, or sing your family's mission statement.

VISION REVIEW

Read your vision statement aloud.

GOAL REVIEW

- What goal(s) are you working toward? ____________________________________

  ____

- Does it still sound reasonable? ____

  ____

- What systems or habits did you put into place to help you make progress? _______

  ____

- How did it go this week? ____

  ____

- What things got in the way of progress this week? What things helped?__________

  ____

- Do you need prompts or reminders? If so, how and where? ____________________

  ____

- What things do you want to celebrate about the process this week? _____________

  ____

- Do you need to change your habits? Do you need to change your goal? __________

  ____

- How can you support one another better next week? ________________________

  ____

DISCOVER YOUR FAITH

Does your family travel internationally? Do you know people in other countries? Or do you wish that you knew more about other places and people?

The Catholic Church is global. It began with the first Christian mission, described in Matthew 10:5–15, when Jesus sent his apostles out to speak about the kingdom of heaven. As Catholics, we're still called to live out a mission today … which is exactly why you've been working so hard this year.

But you don't have to get out your passport (unless you want to). Take a virtual trip with the resources from the Maryknoll Office for Global Concerns. They include downloadable reflection guides and webinars on ecological issues, welcoming the stranger, nonviolence, and more from representatives of the Maryknoll Fathers and Brothers, Maryknoll Sisters, and Maryknoll Lay Missioners.

Maryknoll is the more familiar name for the Catholic Foreign Mission Society of America (for priests and brothers) and the Maryknoll Sisters of St. Dominic. The organization began more than 110 years ago to send missionaries from the US Catholic Church around the world.

Though today the United States has become a destination for Catholic missionaries from places such as Africa, thanks to our declining number of priests and parishioners, Maryknoll still sends religious and laypeople across the globe to work for peace, social justice, and the integrity of creation.

Tailor your "excursion" to your family's interests! You can sort by topics and regions; if you don't already have a connection to a place, grab a globe and choose one. Make it a multisensory, engaging event with music, food, and décor from that region. After all, part of mission work is walking joyfully with the people you serve.

You might decide to sponsor a cause in your destination, offer ongoing prayers, or even plan a real-life journey to see God's work alive in another part of the world. (For the latter, check out the Family Missions Company. YES — you can serve as an entire family!) As a veteran of several mission trips, I promise it will be one of the best adventures you've ever had.

Your family is not working on your faith alone. Your little team is a part of a world full of faithful who are seeking, teaching, and living out the love that Jesus so radically showed us when he died for our sins.

ENCOURAGEMENT

If you feel like you're living parallel lives with your family — all moving forward in the same direction, but without a minute to turn and face one another — it's time to try some team-building exercises.

Science of People (scienceofpeople.com) has published some great ideas in "Twelve Non-Awkward Team Building Activities that Build Trust." You can pick and choose from anything on the list there, but "Use Nostalgia to Build Trust on a Team" is perfect in a family setting. It can help parents recognize their children as individuals and peek inside their internal lives, and it can help children see their parents as individuals and realize that they had a childhood as well.

I credit my guy with teaching me to ask these kinds of questions of my loved ones, and the answers never fail to surprise me. I learn things about my grandparents and parents that I'd never imagine in a million years — little treasures like the fact that one of my grandmothers used to go roller skating, and the other dreamed of being a flight attendant when commercial flight was new.

Don't let this be a one-time practice. You might see your "team" members in a whole new light.

PRAYER

Jesus, you call us to know you through others — those who live around the globe and those who live in our own home. Help us find ways to "practice hospitality ungrudgingly to one another" (1 Peter 4:9). Whenever, wherever, to whomever. Amen!

TEAM SPIRIT

Close out your family meeting with some excitement and joy!

NOTES FOR NEXT TIME

WEEK 49

DATE ____________ TIME______________ PLACE ______________________________

OPENING RITUAL

Remember, parents, this is up to you and your creativity! Is it a song that you sing or listen to together? A "ready-set-go" team chant? A minute of jumping jacks to get out the wiggles? Try out some ways to make your meetings "official" and create a mood of openness and engagement.

PRAYER

Take sixty seconds to pray together. You can pray in silence, or you can recite a traditional prayer such as the Our Father or Hail Mary.

MISSION REVIEW

Ask someone to recite, write, or sing your family's mission statement.

VISION REVIEW

Read your vision statement aloud.

GOAL REVIEW

- What goal(s) are you working toward? ________________________________

  ____

- Does it still sound reasonable? ______________________________________

  ____

- What systems or habits did you put into place to help you make progress? _______

  ____

- How did it go this week? ____

  ____

- What things got in the way of progress this week? What things helped?__________

____

- Do you need prompts or reminders? If so, how and where? ____________________

____

- What things do you want to celebrate about the process this week? ______________

____

- Do you need to change your habits? Do you need to change your goal? __________

____

- How can you support one another better next week? _________________________

____

DISCOVER YOUR FAITH

There's a lot to learn historically, traditionally, and ritually about the Catholic Faith. But if we're only learning and not doing, we can run into a big disconnect with the ever-changing nature of Catholicism as a faith that is alive, active, and growing.

We have a really cool opportunity as US Catholics. The portrait of a "typical" Catholic has been changing. Today, more than 40 percent of Catholics in America are Hispanic; that jumps to about 60 percent of US Catholics younger than eighteen. And while some are immigrants, nearly two-thirds were born here. They are US Catholics in every sense of the word.

As Hosffman Ospino writes, "This is not the first time that US Catholicism has been drastically transformed. The arrival of millions of European immigrants in this country in the 19th and 20th centuries had a similar effect."[56]

The current transformation allows us Catholics in the US to reshape the ways in which we express our faith. There is a vibrancy of family life, an influx of traditions, and an emphasis on parts of Catholicism that those who come from a different cultural background might overlook.

Ways of celebrating can expand to include new foods, new music, new language, or even additional feast days on the parish event schedule. "[Hispanic people] account for 71 percent of the growth of the Catholic population in the United States since 1960," Ospino writes.

The Church has a new demographic breathing life into it; perhaps your family reflects this. This is an opportunity to expand our thinking of "US Catholic" … and a cause to celebrate. The faith of our childhood, the faith of our family is thriving!

For centuries, the Church has lived here on earth as a reflection of the people who have found their identity in Catholicism. Yet she always remains true to the words of Jesus: "Whoever does the will of God is my brother, and sister, and mother" (Mark 3:35).

ENCOURAGEMENT

Have you been using your mission statement to make your life easier?

Yes, I know — this whole process of crafting a mission statement, vision, and goals may have made your life more complicated or busy in some ways.

But at the same time, it's meant to help you distill busyness into the actions that matter. As Sarah Aboulhosn writes, a mission statement "can also be an excellent barometer for determining whether new projects align with your overall brand mission."[57] So remember to use your mission as a tool — not to make longer to-do lists, but to vet them and make sure that the things on them are worthwhile and meaningful.

PRAYER

From the first apostles in the Holy Land, today the Middle East, the Church has grown in many ways. Today, close with the Apostles' Creed in Spanish:

Creo en Dios, Padre todopoderoso, creador del Cielo y de la Tierra.
Creo en Jesucristo su único Hijo, Nuestro Señor,
que fue concebido por obra y gracia del Espíritu Santo;
nació de Santa María Virgen;
padeció bajo el poder de Poncio Pilato;
fue crucificado, muerto y sepultado;
descendió a los infiernos;
al tercer día resucitó de entre los muertos;
subió a los cielos y está a la diestra de Dios Padre;
desde allí ha de venir a juzgar a los vivos y a los muertos.
Creo en el Espíritu Santo, en la Santa Iglesia Católica,
la comunión de los Santos en el perdon de los pecados
la resurrección de los muertos y la vida eterna.
Amén.

TEAM SPIRIT

Close out your family meeting with some excitement and joy!

NOTES FOR NEXT TIME

WEEK 50

DATE ____________ TIME____________ PLACE ______________________________

OPENING RITUAL

Remember, parents, this is up to you and your creativity! Is it a song that you sing or listen to together? A "ready-set-go" team chant? A minute of jumping jacks to get out the wiggles? Try out some ways to make your meetings "official" and create a mood of openness and engagement.

PRAYER

Take sixty seconds to pray together. You can pray in silence, or you can recite a traditional prayer such as the Our Father or Hail Mary.

MISSION REVIEW

Ask someone to recite, write, or sing your family's mission statement.

VISION REVIEW

Read your vision statement aloud.

GOAL REVIEW

- What goal(s) are you working toward? ______________________________

  ____

- Does it still sound reasonable? ______________________________

  ____

- What systems or habits did you put into place to help you make progress? _______

  ____

- How did it go this week? ______________________________

  ____

- What things got in the way of progress this week? What things helped?__________

  ____

- Do you need prompts or reminders? If so, how and where? ____________________

  ____

- What things do you want to celebrate about the process this week? _____________

  ____

- Do you need to change your habits? Do you need to change your goal? __________

  ____

- How can you support one another better next week? _______________________

  ____

DISCOVER YOUR FAITH

When we began "discovering our faith" months ago, we learned about things that some might consider very "Catholic": the Rosary, the sacraments, Sunday Mass, praying to Mary, and other practices that sometimes seem strange to non-Catholics … and even to Catholics who might not remember much from their Sunday school lessons.

Over the past few weeks, we've touched on a lot of topics that might not seem Catholic at all: racism, environmentalism, immigration, differing abilities, and other issues that seem to inflame conversation and lead to more arguing rather than love.

From Catholic ritual to Catholic social teaching, there are many ways to express your Catholic identity within your family. This year you've worked to do so based on your calling, which you've figured out by working on your mission, vision, and goals.

But now that you've been introduced to some perhaps new ways in which to live as Catholics, have your family's mission, vision, or goals changed for next year?

Do you see how your unique team is a vital, welcome, and necessary part of God's family?

And have you experienced the deep peace that comes from knowing you are a part of a culture of love, encouragement, and grace — both in your family here on earth, and your eternal home with the Father?

We are social creatures, designed by God to be a part of something bigger. Ideally, we find that first within our families. But along the way, we're called by God to see others as he sees everyone: part of his family, loved wildly despite our failures, our mistakes, and our sins.

Consider this passage from St. Paul's Letter to the Ephesians (1:5–6): "He destined us in love to be his sons through Jesus Christ, according to the purpose of his will, to the praise of his glorious grace which he freely bestowed on us in the Beloved."

We are so loved that we are chosen to be God's children; our lives are meant to be a constant example of thanks for the grace that he gave us when he sent Jesus to die for our sins, so that we could live with God forever after our lives are over.

Mission, vision, goals? These are ways to structure and implement the really big idea of living lives of praise to God, in the ways that we've been uniquely made and called. Ritual and teaching are ways to understand and express God's incredible, unending love.

ENCOURAGEMENT

This encouragement comes straight from the Bible. Sure, productivity hacks and time-management tricks will help you do hard things when life is really busy (and when is it not really busy?). But the inspiration that comes from God's love — and the knowledge that every person of faith has struggled to live as a constant example of love, thanks, and praise — is hope like no other:

> For this reason I bow my knees before the Father, from whom every family in heaven and on earth is named, that according to the riches of his glory he may grant you to be strengthened with might through his Spirit in the inner man, and that Christ may dwell in your hearts through faith; that you, being rooted and grounded in love, may have power to comprehend with all the saints what is the breadth and length and height and depth, and to know the love of Christ which surpasses knowledge, that you may be filled with all the fulness of God. (Ephesians 3:14–19)

PRAYER

Dear God, even though it's impossible with our limited human experience to really understand how much you love us, thank you. Thanks for your grace, forgiveness, and love, which give us the hope of heaven. Amen.

WEEK 51

DATE ____________ TIME____________ PLACE ______________________________

This week, you near the end of your yearlong adventure! Yeehaw! Instead of your usual program (meeting/soiree/jamboree/get-together — whatever you like to call it), spend this time talking about what you've done, learned, and experienced.

Take turns talking, and make sure that everyone has a chance to answer. Allow time for reflection after each question. Provide pencils and paper so that each person can make notes about his or her answer — it's easy to forget what you wanted to say when you don't go first.

There are no right answers, so encourage honest answers. Every individual's different experience is valid. Remember the rules of engagement with which you started in chapter 4, such as no yucking someone's yums. Record each person's responses in some way, so that you can use this feedback for next year … because ideally, you're going to do this all again!

SOME STARTER QUESTIONS

- What did you think this would be like when we started? How did it measure up to your expectations — was it the same or different?
- What were your top three favorite things about this adventure? And what did you like the least?
- What surprises did you learn about yourself, your family, and the Church?
- What do you still want to learn more about?
- How has your relationship with your family changed? Your relationship with your faith? Your relationship with the Father, the Son, and the Holy Spirit?
- When you do this again, how would you do things differently? What would you do the same?
- Has creating a family mission and vision, setting goals, and working on habits changed other parts of your life?
- What do you most want to remember about the past year?

SOME WAYS TO HONOR YOUR WORK

How do you want to honor the commitment and efforts that you made over the past year? What goals and habits do you want to celebrate? What parts of your vision are more real today than they were when you started? How are your relationships with one another and with Jesus even better than before?

Think about meaningful yet fun activities that you can do next week to recognize the work that you've done, and the work that the Holy Spirit has done through you. You could include some of your favorites from your kickoff party way back when, and you could create new ones. Some suggestions:

- Draw a map, with your family mission from the beginning of the year as the starting point and your vision as today's destination. Plot out the goals that you achieved as your stops along the way. Feel free to include car snacks in this process!
- Assemble a photo album or scrapbook with memorable moments from your adventure. If you have digital photos, you can make a coffee table book with a tool such as Shutterfly.
- Host a party with your neighbors, people in your parish or community, or people whom you met through your work toward your vision. This is a great opportunity to explain what your family has been up to.
- Write thank you cards to one another and to those who helped you along the way.
- Make a video incorporating photos from your past year, and allow each member of your family to contribute a recorded message. VidDay (vidday.com) is an easy and inexpensive tool to help you do this.
- Get dressed up and have a fancy dinner by candlelight. Use the guest china!

Most importantly, include everyone in the planning. Ask for their ideas! You can use a whiteboard, or have each person write a suggestion on a slip of paper and then vote on the top picks, or incorporate everything.

Don't be afraid to be extravagant. Keep in mind that Jesus performed his first public miracle at a wedding feast (see John 2:1–12). And consider how lavishly you are loved by God as his children. Faith should be joyful!

Now use the coming week to prepare what you need for your final family jamboree of the year. If you need two weeks, use two weeks. Give everyone a task and get ready to celebrate!

PRAYER

Dear God,
Thank you!
Thank you for our family here in this room.
Thank you for our brothers and sisters here on Earth.
Thank you for making us your children.
Thank you for offering us unending grace, over and over again.
Thank you for giving us hope to join you in heaven.
Thank you for giving us unique talents and gifts, as well as the courage to answer your call.
We pray that our answer to your call this past year reflects our gratitude and love.
Amen.

NOTES FOR NEXT TIME

WEEK 52

DATE ____________ TIME______________ PLACE ______________________________

OPENING RITUAL

Remember, parents, this is up to you and your creativity! Is it a song that you sing or listen to together? A "ready-set-go" team chant? A minute of jumping jacks to get out the wiggles? Try out some ways to make your meetings "official" and create a mood of openness and engagement.

CELEBRATION

Hooray!

You did it! You completed an entire year of learning about your faith, your family, and your individual gifts. You completed an entire year of service and prayer, planning and motivating, deciding on and doing different things to make your life look more like your vision of your best selves … those selves God created each of you to be.

Did you ever think you'd get here? I did. But I knew it wouldn't be easy, so you should be really proud of yourselves and your team.

Give one another some high fives and pats on the back, and a few hugs. Then pause to praise the One who made this all possible, who loved us so much that he sent his only Son to die on the cross for us:

> Praise the LORD!
> Praise God in his sanctuary;
>   praise him in his mighty firmament!
> Praise him for his mighty deeds;
>   praise him according to his exceeding greatness!
> Praise him with trumpet sound;
>   praise him with lute and harp!
> Praise him with timbrel and dance;
>   praise him with strings and pipe!
> Praise him with sounding cymbals;
>   praise him with loud clashing cymbals!
> Let everything that breathes praise the LORD!
> Praise the LORD! (Psalm 150:1–6)

Now it's time to party!

CONCLUSION

DATE ____________ TIME____________ PLACE ______________________________

OPENING RITUAL

Remember, parents, this is up to you and your creativity! Is it a song that you sing or listen to together? A "ready-set-go" team chant? A minute of jumping jacks to get out the wiggles? Try out some ways to make your meetings "official" and create a mood of openness and engagement.

WHAT'S NEXT?

Are you ready to do it all again?

I hope so. I hope that you've found the past year to be so rewarding and fulfilling that you can't wait to set out on another adventure together.

In the past year, you visited all the stops that I mapped out for you — the places where you could meet your faith. You probably took lots of side trips to places that especially interested your family. And you've come a long way from the plans that you made when you first set out.

So where do you go from here?

Look at your initial mission, vision, and goals. Decide whether they can serve you for another year, or whether you need to tweak or even rewrite them. Kids grow older. Parents grow wiser. (Or we think we do, anyway.) See what fits for the future.

Look back on the things that you wished you could learn more about in the past year. Were there topics you wanted to spend more time on? Make a list. If last year was a world tour, this year is your chance to live like a local in some aspect of your calling.

If you'd like to use someone else's trip plans for your journey in the year ahead, there are lots and lots of curricula and resources to draw upon. A few to check out:

- *Forming Families: A Faith Resource on Catholic Identity*, by Dr. Kathie Amidei (Huntington, IN: OSV, 2019), is written for a parish director of religious education, but it's easily adapted to your family, with age-appropriate lessons and activities.
- *The Pope Francis Family Devotional: 365 Reflections to Share with Your Kids,* edited by Rebecca Vitz Cherico (Huntington, IN: OSV, 2016), is perfect for dinnertime or bedtime — a short daily passage from Pope Francis, with a brief reflection or question for discussion.
- The Alliance for Catholic Education from the University of Notre Dame provides resources that are as easily effective in a family setting as they are in the classroom. There are reflections on Bible verses, seasons and more. Check it out at ace.nd.edu/resources.
- LifeTeen matches the energy that middle schoolers and teens bring to everything, with resources that you can use at home as well as real-world camps and events to

bring Catholic teens together. See https://lifeteen.com.

- College Connection is an online guide for college students and other young adults by Chris Stefanick of Real Life Catholic. You can find it at https://coaching.reallifecatholic.com/college-enroll-now.
- And the *OSV Kids* magazine is great for parents of kids ages two to six, with stories and hands-on learning structured around the liturgical year.

Consider expanding your involvement in community-oriented endeavors that spoke to your family last year. Is there a new or bigger role for your team? If you've found your jam, why not explore how you can do a little more?

Look for the signposts to lead you to your next journey in the year ahead. Examine the detours that were surprise hits. Start from where you are today, and imagine where you want to end up in another fifty-two weeks.

Spend some time in quiet and prayer, listening for God's call and the whispers of the Holy Spirit. Along with your intellectual curiosity or your sense of responsibility, your heart has a say in where the coming year takes you.

Go back to weeks 1 through 10, if it helps. Now that you've done this once, it will be much easier to answer the questions there. You might find that some of the answers are the same … and you might get a huge sense of achievement all over again when you look back at where you started.

At the risk of sounding like a broken record, include everyone in your family in this plan. Humility over hierarchy here! You're in this together. You've got one another's backs. You're a team — a domestic church. That shared identity is a gift that you'll unwrap all your lives.

Consider the example of St. Teresa of Calcutta, also known as Mother Teresa. One of the greatest saintly people of modern times, she regularly made adjustments to her operations in Calcutta. Her personal daily routine changed as the needs of her Missionaries of Charity changed, as her management and diplomatic responsibilities grew. She didn't move to the streets for a year and then go home to Macedonia. This was her life. She lived like a local and found ways to grow her contribution to easing suffering for those sick and alone in the gutters of India.

Any successful company makes adjustments in the same way. Every department is responsible for measuring its progress toward the goals it set at the start of the year. Successes and failures help shape the plan for the coming year. A growth mindset turns misses into learning experiences. And every new goal can be tied back to the mission or vision.

God has put you on this earth for a reason, and he's put you with these people in your family. He has made you a part of his family, and opened the door to life in heaven one day. Why? What are you going to do with that?

Your next adventure is ahead. Pack your bags and grab the snacks. Go live your calling and change the world!

PRAYER

You can read the following passage from the Bible together, or meditate on the closing words of the Mass, or make up a family prayer of your own. Speak to God from your hearts in the way that is most meaningful to you.

> For I know the plans I have for you, says the LORD, plans for welfare and not for evil, to give you a future and a hope. Then you will call upon me and come and pray to me, and I will hear you. You will seek me and find me; when you seek me with all your heart, I will be found by you, says the LORD. (Jeremiah 29:11–14)
>
> And finally, this is my wish for you:
> The LORD bless you and keep you:
> The LORD make his face to shine upon you, and be gracious to you:
> The LORD lift up his countenance upon you, and give you peace. (Numbers 6:24–26)

Acknowledgments

Thanks and love to my parents, Darrell and Sue Will, who taught me the Faith by the way they lived. My mom's sense of responsibility for her fellow man and my dad's thirst for justice continue to inspire and drive me. (I miss you, Dad.)

And thanks and love to my daughter, Mia, who miraculously grew into a tender, loving adult, despite my harried parenting, and who has given me a second chance to be a tender, loving mother. You are my team.

Notes

INTRODUCTION

1. Julie Hanlon Rubio, "Focusing on Families: Nurturing Catholic Identity and Promoting Social Change through Family Practices," in *Renewing Catholic Family Life: Experts Explore New Directions in Family Spirituality and Family Ministry*, ed. Gregory K. Popcak, Ph.D. (Huntington, IN: OSV, 2020), 97.

THE BEST LAID PLANS

1. Francis, *Lumen Fidei*, Vatican.va, par. 53.

2. "Franklin Covey Habit 3: Put First Things First," FranklinCovey.com, https://www.franklincovey.com/the-7-habits/habit-3/.

3. Carol Dweck, "What Having a 'Growth Mindset' Actually Means," *Harvard Business Review*, January 13, 2016, https://hbr.org/2016/01/what-having-a-growth-mindset-actually-means.

4. Check out Carol S. Dweck, "The Power of Yet," TEDx Norrköping, September 12, 2014, https://youtu.be/J-swZaKN2Ic.

5. Kory Kogon, "2 Tips For Your 2020 New Year's Goals & Resolutions," FranklinCovey, https://resources.franklincovey.com/blog/2-tips-for-your-2020-new-year-s-goals-resolutions.

6. "3-2-1: On the power of simple ideas, focus, and asking good questions," JamesClear.com, July 30, 2020, https://jamesclear.com/3-2-1/july-30-2020.

DID YOU KNOW YOUR FAMILY IS CHURCH?

1. The Second Vatican Council was originally the brainchild of Pope St. John XXIII, who in 1959 announced a plan for a meeting of the minds to develop a Christian and Catholic response to the vast social and cultural changes of the preceding fifty years. Unfortunately, he died just as the second part of the process was beginning in June 1963. Pope St. Paul VI saw the council through to completion in December 1965. It was significant for, among other things, the guidance issued by the Church for everyday Catholics on how to interact with the world. For more information on the council, see Vincenzo Carbone, "Vatican Council II: Light for the Church and the Modern World," http://www.vatican.va/jubilee_2000/magazine/documents/ju_mag_01051997_p-21_en.html.

2. Second Vatican Council, *Lumen Gentium*, ch. 2, no. 11.

3. Timothy O'Malley, in *Renewing Catholic Family Life: Experts Explore New Directions in Family Spirituality and Family Ministry*, ed. Gregory K. Popcak, Ph.D. (Huntington, IN: Our Sunday Visitor, 2020), 31.

4. Julie Hanlon Rubio, "Focusing on Families: Nurturing Catholic Identity and Promoting Social Change through Family Practices," in *Renewing Catholic Family Life: Experts Explore New Directions in Family Spirituality and Family Ministry*, ed. Gregory K. Popcak, Ph.D. (Huntington, IN: OSV, 2019), 106.

5. John Paul II, *Familiaris Consortio*, Vatican.va, par. 17.

6. Francis, *Amoris Laetitia*, Vatican.va, par. 323.

7. Francis, *Fratelli Tutti,* Vatican.va.

A FEW QUICK DEFINITIONS

1. Patagonia.com, "How We're Reducing Our Carbon Footprint," https://www.patagonia.com/stories/how-were-reducing-our-carbon-footprint/story-74099.html.

WE'RE ALL FRIENDS HERE

1. Kristi Hedges, "How To Get Real Buy-In For Your Idea," *Forbes*, March 16, 2015, https://www.forbes.com/sites/work-in-progress/2015/03/16/how-to-get-real-buy-in-for-your-idea/#2ab8cebc4044.

2. Annie Murphy Paul, "How to Get — and Keep — Someone's Attention," *Time* magazine, July 25, 2012, https://ideas.time.com/2012/07/25/how-to-get-and-keep-someones-attention/.

3. Joseph White, *Involving Parents, Engaging Families: Tested Tips for Catechists and Teachers* (Huntington, IN: Our Sunday Visitor, 2015).

4. Did you know that only certain versions of the Bible are Catholic? This book uses The Catholic Edition of the *Revised Standard Version*. For tips on choosing and using a Bible, see the very short article "Understanding the Bible," by Mary Elizabeth Sperry, on the U.S. Conference of Catholic Bishops website, 2023, https://www.usccb.org/bible/understanding-the-bible.

5. *Catechism of the Catholic Church*, Part Three: Life In Christ, Section Two: The Ten Commandments. See also, Exodus 20:2–17 and Deuteronomy 5:6–21.

WEEKS 1-52

1. Simon Sinek, "The Science of WHY," LinkedIn.com, November 16, 2017, https://www.linkedin.com/pulse/science-why-simon-sinek/.

2. John Paul II, *FC,* Vatican.va, par. 17.

3. Chris Drew, "47 Best Talent Examples in a List," helpfulprofessor.com/talent-examples-list.

4. Visit TheHappinessTrap.com to download "The Complete Worksheets for the Confidence Gap." Dr. Russ Harris's list of values starts on page 3 of that PDF, https://thehappinesstrap.com/the-confidence-gap-worksheets/.

5. "The Best Way to Teach Values to Kids, According to Research," *Education Week,* November 11, 2020.

6. Modified from "Managing Employee Surveys," Society for Human Resource Management, https://www.shrm.org/resourcesandtools/tools-and-samples/toolkits/pages/managingemployeesurveys.aspx.

7. Sarah Aboulhosn, "What is a brand mission and how to define it," Sprout Social, August 24, 2020, https://sproutsocial.com/insights/brand-mission/.

8. United States Conference of Catholic Bishops, "Concluding Rights," 2023, https://www.usccb.org/prayer-and-worship/the-mass/order-of-mass/concluding-rites.

9. Kaki Okumura, "Why You Should Write Notes to Your Future Self," Medium.com, November 7, 2018, https://forge.medium.com/a-guide-to-overcoming-your-doubts-and-anxieties-by-writing-to-yourself-cd5714c82f15.

10. Dana G. Smith, "Habits Are the New Resolutions," Elemental, January 5, 2021, 2023, https://elemental.medium.com/habits-are-the-new-resolutions-f168a9b54102.

11. Deep Patel, "Why Perfection Is the Enemy of Done," *Forbes,* June 16, 2017, https://www.forbes.com/sites/deeppatel/2017/06/16/why-perfection-is-the-enemy-of-done/?sh=21d029954395.

12. Mike Sturm, "A Universal Formula for Doing Big Things," Medium.com, May 13, 2020, https://forge.medium.com/the-mvm-a-simple-way-to-break-through-barriers-achieve-big-goals-and-build-good-habits-6f7828353a57.

13. Rachel Hollis, "This Daily Practice Changed My Life and My Business," *RISE* podcast, episode 72, November 2018, https://open.spotify.com/episode/1HsJHoPxWVSRTNoRNB43RF#_=_.

14. Laura Vanderkam, "3 Times a Week Is a Habit," Forge, March 5, 2020, a https://forge.medium.com/3-times-a-week-is-a-habit-b6185dba7c5.

15. Ryan Holiday, "It's Not About Routine, but About Practice," Forge, August 16, 2020, 2023, https://forge.medium.com/its-not-about-routine-but-about-practice-200a56c5505.

16. James Clear, *Atomic Habits: An Easy and Proven Way to Build Good Habits & Break Bad Ones* (New York: Avery, 2018).

17. Francis, *Evangelii Gaudium*, Vatican.va., par. 283.

18. Joan Rosenberg, "What Makes It So Hard to Ask for Help?" *Psychology Today*, April 2, 2019, https://www.psychologytoday.com/us/blog/emotional-mastery/201904/what-makes-it-so-hard-ask-help.

19. James Clear, *The 3-2-1 Newsletter*, August 27, 2020.

20. "Celebrating Achievement," MindTools.com, https://www.mindtools.com/pages/article/celebrating-achievement.htm.

21. United States Conference of Catholic Bishops, "Sacraments and Sacramentals," https://www.usccb.org/prayer-and-worship/sacraments-and-sacramentals.

22. Catholic News Agency, "An Easter Sermon from St. John Chrysostom," https://www.catholicnewsagency.com/resource/55479/an-easter-sermon-from-st-john-chrysostom.

23. Stephen Shedletzky, "Great Leaders and Organizations Advance a Just Cause," 2020, https://simonsinek.com/discover/great-leaders-organizations-advance-a-just-cause/.

24. For a deep dive, see Part 3, section 2, chapter 2, article 4.

25. Courtney Mares, "Pope Francis Calls for a Commitment to 'Take Care of Each Other' in 2021," Angelus News, https://angelusnews.com/news/vatican/pope-francis-calls-for-a-commitment-to-take-care-of-each-other-in-2021/.

26. Simon Sinek, "We Need More Leaders," https://simonsinek.com/discover/we-need-more-leaders/.

27. Simon Sinek, *Leaders Eat Last: Why Some Teams Pull Together and Others Don't* (NY: Portfolio, 2014).

28. Francis, *Fratelli Tutti*, Vatican.va.

29. O'Malley in *Renewing Catholic Family Life*, 42.

30. Ibid., 43.

31. Visit https://www.usccb.org/offices/justice-peace-human-development/forming-consciences-faithful-citizenship.

32. *Compendium of the Social Doctrine of the Church*, no. 201, Vatican.va.

33. Simon Sinek, "Find Your WHY," SimonSinek.com, https://simonsinek.com/commit/why-discovery-course-intro/.

34. Lisa Marie Segarra, "Read What Pope Francis Said About Power and Humility at Surprise TED Talk," *TIME*, April 26, 2017, https://time.com/4755663/pope-francis-ted-talk-transcript/.

35. Francis, "Why the Only Future Worth Building Includes Everyone," trans. Elena Montrasio, April 2017, https://www.ted.com/talks/his_holiness_pope_francis_why_the_only_future_worth_building_includes_everyone.

36. "Shirley Young: Market Research Pioneer," BillMoyers.com, March 1, 2003, https://billmoyers.com/content/shirley-young/.

37. Herbert Lui, "To Stick to Your New Year's Resolution, Get It Out of Your Head," Forge, January 2, 2020, https://forge.medium.com/to-stick-to-your-new-years-resolution-get-it-out-of-your-head-f917f8816bfa.

38. See "Seven Themes of Catholic Social Teaching," USCCB, https://www.usccb.org/beliefs-and-teachings/what-we-believe/catholic-social-teaching/seven-themes-of-catholic-social-teaching.

39. Sharlyn Lauby, "Interview: Dr. John Kotter on Creating Organizational Change," *HR Bartender,* November 13, 2011, https://www.hrbartender.com/2011/business-and-customers/interview-dr-john-kotter-on-creating-organizational-change/.

40. "How to Motivate Children: Science-Based Approaches for Parents, Caregivers, and Teachers," Harvard University, Center on the Developing Child, https://developingchild.harvard.edu/resources/how-to-motivate-children-science-based-approaches-for-parents-caregivers-and-teachers/.

41. "Open Wide Our Hearts: The Enduring Call to Love — A Pastoral Letter Against Racism," Committee on Cultural Diversity in the Church of the United States Conference of Catholic Bishops (USCCB). © 2018, United States Conference of Catholic Bishops, Washington, DC. All rights reserved. https://www.usccb.org/issues-and-action/human-life-and-dignity/racism/upload/open-wide-our-hearts.pdf.

42. Ibid.

43. Therese Perby Señal, "Beyond the Wall: Human Impacts, Moral Principles, and Policy Directions on Immigration," February 14, 2019, https://catholicsocialthought.georgetown.edu/posts/beyond-the-wall-human-impacts-moral-principles-and-policy-directions-on-immigration.

44. United States Conference of Catholic Bishops, "Situation at the U.S.-Mexico Border," 2023, https://www.usccb.org/news/2021/situation-us-mexico-border.

45. Gene Hammett, "You're Setting Goals All Wrong. Here's the Process You Should Be Using," Inc.com, January 24, 2019, https://www.inc.com/gene-hammett/how-to-better-set-your-goals-in-2019.html.

46. James Clear, *Atomic Habits*, 15.

47. Catholic Climate Covenant, "Our Story," https://catholicclimatecovenant.org/about/story.

48. Francis, *Our Mother Earth: A Christian Reading of the Challenge of the Environment* (Huntington, IN: OSV, 2019), 34.

49. "Women in Innovation: NASA's Dr. Ellen Ochoa," USPTOvideo, at https://youtu.be/ZnMYy_wHk1s.

50. Benedict XVI, *Caritas in Veritate*, Vatican.va.

51. Francis, *Laudato Sí*, Vatican.va, par. 146

52. Judith Valente, "Native American Catholics Reconcile the Past and Future," *U.S. Catholic*, April 23, 2019, https://uscatholic.org/articles/201904/native-american-catholics-are-reconciling-their-past-and-future/.

53. "Message of the Holy Father Francis for the International Day of Persons with Disabilities," December 3, 2020, Vatican.va.

54. Francis, *Gaudete et Exsultate,* Vatican.va., par. 101.

55. Francis, *Fratelli Tutti,* Vatican.va., par. 118.

56. "10 Ways Hispanics Are Redefining American Catholicism in the 21st Century," *America*, November 13, 2017, https://www.americamagazine.org/faith/2017/10/30/10-ways-hispanics-are-redefining-american-catholicism-21st-century.

57. Sarah Aboulhosn, "What is a brand mission and how to define it," SproutSocial.com, August 24, 2020, https://sproutsocial.com/insights/brand-mission/.

About the Author

Julianne Will is an accomplished copywriter and content strategist, with a long career in journalism, advertising, and publishing. She has authored several children's books for OSV, including the *Catholic Prayer Book for Children*, which spent nineteen months on the National Catholic Book Publishers Association's youth bestseller list. An avid traveler and outdoor enthusiast, Julianne lives in Denver and spends as much time with her lovely daughter as possible.

You might also like:

Catholic Prayer Book for Children

By Julianne M. Will

With colorful, captivating illustrations, the ***Catholic Prayer Book for Children*** helps children ages 6 and up discover the beauty of prayer as it encourages them to form the lifelong habit of praying.

Beloved, traditional Catholic prayers are included, along with the basics of the Catholic Faith like the Ten Commandments, Beatitudes, sacraments, corporal and spiritual works of mercy, an age-appropriate "examination of conscience," and an introduction to the Mass.